AMERICA'S BEST CHEFS COOK *with*

Jeremiah TOWER

AMERICA'S BEST CHEFS COOK *with*

Jeremiah TOWER

Jeremiah Tower

COMPANION TO THE PBS TELEVISION
SERIES OF THE SAME NAME PRODUCED BY
SANTA FE VENTURES, INC.

WILEY

John Wiley & Sons, Inc.

Copyright © 2003 by Jeremiah Tower and Santa Fe Ventures, Inc. All rights reserved

Published by John Wiley & Sons, Inc., Hoboken, New Jersey

Published simultaneously in Canada

For general information on our other products and services or for technical support, please contact our Customer Care Department within the United States at (800) 762-2974, outside the United States at (317) 572-3993 or fax (317) 572-4002.

Wiley also publishes its books in a variety of electronic formats. Some content that appears in print may not be available in electronic books. For more information about Wiley products, visit our web site at www.wiley.com.

Library of Congress Cataloging-in-Publication Data:

Tower, Jeremiah.
    America's best chefs cook with Jeremiah Tower / Jeremiah Tower.
        p. cm.
Includes index.
    ISBN 0-471-45141-X (Cloth)
    1. Cookery, American. I. Title.

TX715 .T7383 2003
641.5973—dc21   2003007453

Printed in the United States of America

10 9 8 7 6 5 4 3 2 1

Contents

Introduction

The saying of a nineteenth-century French gourmet from Brittany has fared better than his current reputation as a philosopher: "The most charming hours of our life are connected with a memory of the table." Another Frenchman, whose name around the world has fared better than any of his sayings other than "keep it simple," echoes the first: "Good cooking is the basis of true happiness."

Jeremiah Tower on location in San Francisco (above) and studying notes (at left).

I have found that America's best chefs all have in common their agreement with Monselet and Escoffier, the two distinguished gentlemen referred to above. The first sentiment is what got them to their stoves in the first place; and the second is what keeps them going and makes them stay there—along with one of those obscure proverbs that he/she gives nothing who does not give himself/herself. Their constant giving is what makes them the best.

James Beard, a true lover of French or any kind of good cooking, was in love particularly with traditional and regional American food, from the simple to the most luxurious. At the age of sixty-five he concluded, in *American Cookery* (1972), that American cooking was one of the most fascinating styles of all. The selection of the chefs for this book was done by the James Beard Foundation, using the winners of the regional awards (ten of those) as well as (Best) Outstanding Restaurant in America, Best New Restaurant, and Best Pastry Chef. If Beard saw a renaissance happening in the American culinary scene, then these names are its princes and princesses.

In the seventies, James Beard and I had talked many times about what he called the current "crossroads between technology and tradition" in American cookery. As I went around the United States visiting these chefs on their home ground, I was impressed by their commonly demonstrated sure-handedness with all the new ingredients whose newness had tripped up so many creative chefs in the eighties. Thirty years later, it is clear that America's best chefs have fused the two roads into one main highway. The revolution in the way America eats has succeeded, and the chefs in this book are leading the way to the next one.

All the food was cooked in All-Clad Metalcrafters cookware, sent to each of the chefs by this sponsoring company. I think that everyone agreed the pans had perfect temperature dispersion, a fact that half of them had already figured out: they had the pans hanging in their houses or restaurants. I have used this cookware for years, but only on this trip visiting all the chefs was I able to test the absolutely brilliant new "metal-sandwich" pots with stainless steel on both exterior surfaces with copper in the center. All the benefits of copper and none of the polishing!

The recipes were taken from the tapes of the PBS television series "America's Best Chefs," which we filmed on the road with these chefs, from my notes that I took while cooking with them, from still photographs, and from the recipes sent to me by them. Certainly one of the common themes in the interviews and televised footage of the chefs is that all of them were eager to make the same point about recipes: easily master these recipes, and then use them as a guideline in your cooking. Charlie Trotter particularly says that on any given day in his restaurant, a particular dish may differ depending on what is at hand or what they have learned from cooking the recipe several times over a period of days. Robert McGrath saw his recipes as inspirational guidelines for cooking his dishes at home with endless variations. What we cooked for the cameras often were variations on the recipes we were handed; so here I have written recipes that for me best represent the spirit of the dish I saw as well as the written recipe.

And perhaps that is the clue to what makes the "Best": a cook forever in love with what he or she is doing, and forever seeking to improve what is put on the table. Certainly, on this trip I saw only happy chefs.

America's Best Chefs Cook *with* Jeremiah Tower

About the Chefs

Philippe Boulot

As a 1978 graduate of the Jean Drouant Hotel School in Paris, Boulot's desire to travel and work in the world's finest hotels took him to The Nikko in Paris, Four Seasons Inn on The Park in London, Four Seasons Cliff Hotel in San Francisco, and the Mark hotel in New York. At the Mark Hotel, he was the opening chef, and *Gourmet*'s former restaurant critic, Andy Birsch, for one, was mightily impressed. "If credit were given where credit is due," wrote Birsch, "then Mark's restaurant might be named Philippe's, for it is the province of a young and capable French chef, Philippe Boulot."

Captivated by the quality of life and the diversity of local ingredients available in the Pacific Northwest, Philippe Boulot moved to Portland, Oregon, to join the historic Heathman Hotel restaurant in April of 1994. A rising star of the 1990s, Boulot's significant culinary strengths have added to Portland's growing reputation as an international food destination. Striving for "freshness, flavor, and truthful presentation on every plate," Boulot's French Northwest cuisine is a marriage of traditional French training with contemporary sensibilities, using the finest seasonal ingredients on the market.

Philippe Boulot grew up in the Normandy region in France making butter and cheese as a young child with his grandmother. At sixteen, he stepped into the professional ring, apprenticing with some of France's most acclaimed chefs, including Joël Robuchon at Jamin and Alain Senderens at L'Archestrate in Paris.

As executive chef of The Heathman Restaurant, Chef Boulot and his talented kitchen staff have earned The Heathman a number of awards over the years, including the 1997 Fine Dining Hall of Fame Award from *Nation's Restaurant News*, *Gourmet* magazine's 1997 honor as one of the Top 10 Tables in Portland, one of Condé Nast's Top 250 Restaurants in America in 1995, and the *Zagat Survey* Award in 1997. Most recently, Chef Boulot was honored as a James Beard Award nominee for Best Chef in the Northwest for 2002.

Chef Boulot exposes Oregonians to new and exciting cuisine throughout the year. Menus change seasonally to showcase the natural bounty of the Pacific Northwest, and special dishes are offered daily. Through his "Philippe's Friends" program, Chef Boulot brings world-renowned chefs to The Heathman Restaurant & Bar to share their expertise.

Over the years, Chef Boulot has hosted the likes of chefs Angelo "Balin" Silvestro, Michel Brunel, and André Soltner of Lutèce (New York) fame. Visiting chefs join Chef Boulot in developing special prix-fixe menus for restaurant patrons. Chef Boulot, in turn, takes his culinary gifts to various venues around the country, such as the James Beard House and The Mark in New York.

Alain Ducasse

Photo © M. Rougemont

When Alain Ducasse announced the opening of Alain Ducasse at the Essex House in New York, he set the restaurant world abuzz. The internationally renowned chef of four Michelin-starred restaurants in Paris, Monte Carlo, and Provence was entering the American market with a bang. The media frenzy surrounding the restaurant's opening was huge. With only 65 seats and one sitting per evening of 3- to 6-course prix-fixe tasting menus (starting at $150 per person), Ducasse let New Yorkers know that a serious new dining experience had arrived. Ducasse's gamble paid off. *The New York Times* bestowed a four-star review. The James Beard Foundation's "Best New Restaurant of 2000" followed. In 2001, *Condé Nast Traveler* called it one of its "100 Hot Tables," and *Bon Appétit* named Ducasse "Chef of the Year." The accolades continued with Alain Ducasse at the Essex House receiving Mobil Guide's only new Five-Star Award and the AAA's 2002 Five-Diamonds Award. And most recently, *GQ* magazine honored Ducasse as part of their Men of the Year feature under the title "Chef."

Ducasse's culinary vision is international; it began in 1987 when he became Chef des Cuisines at Le Louis XV restaurant at the Hotel de Paris in Monte Carlo—the first hotel restaurant to be awarded three stars in the Michelin Red Guide. In typical Ducasse fashion, he accepted a contractual challenge to win three stars within four years. Le Louis XV is one of the most luxurious hotel restaurants in the world. In 1996, Ducasse captured the hearts of Parisian gourmands with the opening of Alain Ducasse restaurant in Le Parc-Sofitel Demeure Hôtels. Eight months later, the restaurant received three stars from the Red Guide. It later moved to the Hotel Plaza Athéné in 2000, and five months later its excellence was reconfirmed with three Michelin stars.

Not content with three demanding and celebrated dining establishments, Ducasse's energies have been engaged in managing luxurious inns, beginning in 1995 with La Bastide de Moustiers, a twelve-bedroom country inn near the Verdon Gorges in Provence. The inn's restaurant received its one star in the Red Guide in 2002. With a friend, Clement Bruno, he also opened L'Hostellerie de l'Abbaye de la Celle, an eighteenth-century mansion boasting ten bedrooms.

Ducasse has also devoted his energies to creating a concept restaurant. Spoon Food & Wine opened in Paris in 1998. The idea was that a diner could create their own meal by choosing entrees, condiments, and garnishes, which would be cooked in a number of ways. The idea was adapted successfully for Spoon des Iles in Saint Gerain, Spoon + at Sanderson in London, Spoon Food & Wine in Japan, and Spoon Byblos in St. Tropez. Ducasse's culinary empire also extends to two other Paris-based restaurants: 59 Poincare, specializing in four ingredients—vegetables, lobster, beef, and fruit; and Il Cortile, an Italian restaurant with a contemporary approach to food from all that country's regions. Il Cortile is also the recipient of a star in the Red Guide. Finally, Ducasse has established *bar & boeuf* restaurant bar in Monte Carlo. Here diners are offered an infinite variety of ways to eat sea bass and beef, from the traditional to the contemporary. Again the Ducasse imprimatur has resulted in a Michelin star.

Last summer Ducasse opened Auberge Iparla in the French Basque country, and Aux Lyonnais opened in Paris in October 2002.

Born on a farm in Castelsarrazin in the Landes region of southwestern France, Alain Ducasse was raised surrounded by pullets, ducks and geese, boletus mushrooms, and foie gras. His passion for cooking was established early in his youth and he began his training as an apprentice at the Bordeaux hotel school. Ambitious and eager to learn from the masters, he "forced" his way into Michel Guérard's restaurant in Eugéne-les-Bains where he remained for two years, except for a few winter periods working for pastry legend Gaston Lenôtre. In 1978, Ducasse went to work for Alain Chapel in Mionnay. He spent two years there, and considers Chapel to be his spiritual master. Roger Vergé, another legendary French chef, offered him the position of Chef at L'Amandier, in Mougins. One year later, Ducasse took charge of the kitchen brigade at La Terrasse, the restaurant in the Hôtel Juana in Juan-les-Pins. In 1984, he was awarded his first two stars in the Michelin Red Guide. He was only thirty. The extraordinary achievement of Le Louis XV was only two years away.

Gale Gand

Awards & Honors

TRU

2001   James Beard Foundation, Dolce Outstanding Pastry Chef of the Year

2000   James Beard Foundation, Nominated for Outstanding Pastry Chef

1997   Finalist for the Julia Child Cookbook Awards through the International Association of Culinary Professionals for *American Brasserie*

1994   Robert Mondavi Award for Culinary Excellence; Rising Star Chefs Award

1994   *Food & Wine* magazine, Top 10 Best New Chefs

1991   Michelin Red "M"

1987   First place in the Heart Healthy Desserts Competition held by the Chicago Heart Association

In the past few years, the dessert chef of a great restaurant has become very important, and one of the very best desserts chefs in America is Gale Gand, who is pastry chef and co-owner with Rick Tramonto (and Rich Melman), of Chicago's acclaimed and award-winning TRU restaurant. Opened just three year ago, TRU has risen to the top ranks of great American dining establishments, and Gale Gand's desserts are praised by all. Pat Bruno, restaurant critic for the *Chicago Sun-Times*, has lauded Gand as "one of the best pastry chefs in the United States," and John Mariani, *Esquire*'s discerning food columnist, was rhapsodic: "Every dessert I tried was poetic. They should be: They are made by the city's best pastry chef, Gale Gand." *The New York Times*' November 1999 review was a rave, including the desserts. "Ms. Gand's seasonal fruit creations are excellent, and she revels in humorous plays on American sweets. Pairing a gooey chocolate fudge tart and caramelized banana with cabernet caramel sauce and peanut butter ice cream to evoke peanut butter and jelly, she elevates quintessential childhood flavors to a high-wire act. But, then, the whole experience at TRU is a culinary Cirque du Soleil."

A native of Chicago's North Shore, Gale Gand has always been an artist. She spent her college years studying silver and goldsmithing. When she took a year off and went to work in a restaurant, she discovered that the skills she had learned in art translated well to cuisine. She started her own catering company and also worked three years at the Strathallen Hotel in Rochester, New York. It was there that she met chef and mentor Greg Broman and future partner Rick Tramonto.

Gand traveled to Europe twice during this period, taking pastry classes at La Varenne in Paris while she experienced the foods of France. In 1985, Gand and Tramonto moved to New York and started at the top in one of the city's most exciting restaurants—Jonathan Waxman's Jams. Her next stint was at Gotham Bar & Grill, where Bryan Miller, restaurant critic of *The New York Times*, awarded her desserts three stars.

Anxious to return to Chicago, Gand took a job at Carlos' Restaurant in Highland Park in 1987. That same year she won first place in the Heart Healthy Desserts Competition held by the Chicago Heart Association. Her next move was to become pastry chef at the Pump Room. Gand opened a series of new restaurants in Chicago as a pastry chef, including Café 21, Bice, and Bella Luna, at which point William Rice, food columnist of the *Chicago Tribune,* dubbed her "Dessert Diva." *Food & Wine* magazine listed her among "People to Watch" for 1989.

While she was pastry chef at Bice, Gand was approached by Bob Payton, who operated fourteen American-style restaurants in London and seventeen other ventures across Europe. Payton asked Gand and Tramonto to transform the kitchen and cuisine at Stapleford Park, a five-star hotel in Leicestershire, some 90 minutes from London. They accepted the challenge, and overcoming some initial skepticism from critics and public alike, Stapleford Park received acclaim from some of London's toughest critics. Fay Maschler of the *London Evening Standard* called Gand's ice creams "the best I have tasted in Britain." Gand was delighted to receive the red "M" in the 1991 Michelin guide, the first received by an American in more than five years.

Back home in Chicago, Gand joined Charlie Trotter's, the four-star restaurant, but then joined Tramonto and Henry Adaniya to open Trio. It was the first new restaurant in Chicago to receive a four-star rating from the *Chicago Tribune* critic Phil Vettel since 1988. After two years, Gand and Tramonto opened Brasserie T, serving robust French/American food in Northfield, Illinois. They closed it in 2001 to concentrate their creative energies on TRU, cookbooks, and television. Gand also began to manufacture and distribute her own brand of root beer, called "Gale's."

Gale Gand is author and co-author of several cookbooks, including *Gale Gand's Just a Bite: 125 Luscious, Little Desserts* (with Julia Moskin), *American Brasserie: 180 Simple, Robust Recipes Inspired by the Rustic Foods of France, Italy and America* (with Rick Tramonto and Julia Moskin), and *Butter Sugar Flour Eggs: Whimsical Irresistible Desserts* (with Rick Tramonto and Julia Moskin).

Jean-Marie Lacroix

"Jean-Marie Lacroix," wrote John Mariani in *Wine Spectator*, is "the white-haired paterfamilias of Philadelphia gastronomy." Since 1983, Lacroix has been teaching Philadelphia foodies what really fine French dining is all about. He's earned rave reviews from just about every food reviewer across the country (plus such accolades as a *Wine Spectator* Best Award of Excellence and a berth in the *Nation's Restaurant News* Fine Dining Hall of Fame). For nearly 20 years, Lacroix helmed kitchens at the Fountain Restaurant of The Four Seasons in Philadelphia. It became a de facto training program for a generation of top young Philadelphia culinarians. Tony Clark, Bruce Lim, Francesco Martorella, Jean-François Taquet, and Martin Hamann all credit him with transforming the city's culinary scene.

It's easy to see why Lacroix has been so influential. As Rebecca Ynocencio wrote in *Gourmet* magazine, "Lacroix's style strikes that often difficult balance between simplicity and grand ambition." It's an equilibrium that French-born Lacroix perfected over a long culinary career, which began at Thonon-les-Bains on Lake Geneva and encompassed stops at a medley of top restaurants and hotels in France, Switzerland, England, Scotland, and Canada. During his tenure at the Fountain, Lacroix earned a slew of honors and awards, including the Philadelphia's Top Table nod from *Gourmet*, five consecutive DiRoNA awards, a spot in *Food & Wine*'s "Top 25 Restaurants in America," an AAA Five-Diamond Award, and the number-two spot in *Condé Nast Traveler's* national reader's poll.

After retiring from the Fountain Restaurant in the fall of 2001, he became the Executive Chef of the Rittenhouse Hotel in Philadelphia, overseeing the kitchen serving the hotel and restaurant, including banquet and room service functions. He also held the position of Master Culinaire in Residence at the Restaurant School at Walnut Hill College and served on the board of the Culinary Arts Program of the Philadelphia Art Alliance.

Awards & Honors

Lacroix at The Rittenhouse

Wine Spectator Best Award of Excellence

Nation's Restaurant News Fine Dining Hall of Fame

Gourmet magazine's Top Table

Five consecutive DiRoNA awards

Food & Wine magazine, Top 25 Restaurants in America

AAA Five-Diamonds Award

Number-two spot in *Condé Nast Traveler*'s national reader's poll

Maitres Cuisiniers de France

James Beard Foundation, Best Chef—Mid-Atlantic

Robert Mondavi Award for Culinary Excellence

Robert McGrath

Robert McGrath has overcome more than a few obstacles on his path to becoming a chef. First there were his parents, who were less than pleased when their son quit college—abandoning a future career as a biochemist—to go to Jamaica and apprentice at a restaurant. As McGrath recalls, "They were ready to disown me." As if the cold shoulder from his parents wasn't enough, he got hazed pretty badly during the early days of his next apprenticeship, this time in France. The chef asked McGrath to make him lunch, and when the eager lad brought it over to him, the chef put the plate down on the floor and called his dog to come and eat it. Ouch! But none of that broke McGrath's spirit.

Living in Florida and Texas, McGrath was exposed to a wide array of foods. Studying in Europe helped McGrath learn the culinary fundamentals. But it has been his unique way of blending these influences with his own distinct and inventive style that has placed him among the most celebrated chefs in America. Following a seven-year stint as executive chef of Windows on the Green at the Phoenician in Scottsdale, McGrath left to open Roaring Fork, and he became a pioneer in the current movement of American western cuisine.

Roaring Fork restaurant blends rustic culinary traditions with contemporary sophistication to create a unique down-home yet elegant dining experience. Colman Andrews, *Saveur* magazine's editor-in-chief, has been enthusiastic about McGrath's skills. "You've got to love a chef like Robert McGrath," he wrote, "who mixes high and low, uptown and down-home, old and new with casual flair and unflagging energy—just like the American West."

McGrath, a native of Kentucky, graduated from the Culinary Institute of America and Le Cordon Bleu in Paris. He was the opening chef of the Four Seasons Hotel in Austin, Texas, after which he moved to its Houston location, where he opened the critically acclaimed DeVille. In 1989, John Mariani tapped DeVille as "one of the Best New Restaurants in

Awards & Honors
Roaring Fork

2001 James Beard Foundation, Best Chef—Southwest

Six previous nominations as Best Chef—Southwest, by the James Beard Foundation

1990 Chefs of America, Chef of the Year

1988 *Food & Wine* magazine, Best New Chef in America

America." McGrath went on to become chef de cuisine at the Scottsdale Princess in Arizona, and from there to his long tenure at the nearby Windows on the Green.

McGrath's success has been recognized by the James Beard Foundation, which has nominated him as one of the best chefs in the southwestern United States seven times. Over the years McGrath has received several other awards, including being selected by *Food & Wine* magazine as one of the Best New Chefs in America in 1988 and, in 1990, being named "Chef of the Year" by his peers at Chefs of America. His talents were again honored in 1991 when, at the request of the White House, McGrath organized and executed dinners for the heads of state attending the Economic Summit for Industrialized Nations in Houston.

McGrath has been inducted into Arizona's Culinary Hall of Fame and has made numerous appearances on national television, including the *Today Show*, *Good Morning America*, and the Food Network, and has been recognized by a number of publications, including *Gourmet* and *Esquire*.

In 1997, McGrath opened Roaring Fork, named after the river in Colorado where he goes fishing every year. The cuisine is of the American West, focusing on ingredients from the Rocky Mountains, the Pacific Northwest, and the California coast, blending rustic culinary traditions with contemporary flourishes. *Food & Wine* calls it "elevated cowboy food that's eminently approachable." McGrath is also the author of *American Western Cooking: From the Roaring Fork*.

In 2001, the seven-time nominee for Best Chef: Southwest finally snagged his James Beard Award.

Nancy Oakes

When Boulevard Restaurant opened in 1993, Chef Nancy Oakes grabbed the affections of San Francisco's diners, who have designated the restaurant the city's most popular. Indeed, Boulevard has been rated the Bay Area's most popular dining destination by *Zagat Survey*, San Francisco every year since 1998. "Nancy Oakes recreates the rich, American cuisine of her L'Avenue on a grand scale, in a setting filled with gorgeous neo-Art Nouveau objects," raved the *San Jose Mercury News*. "Boulevard has been jammed from opening day with people, happy fans devouring maple-cured spit roasted pork loin in a cider sauce, steamed mussels in a tomato broth, corn cakes layered with crab salad and caviar, osso bucco," they happily concluded. *Bon Appetit* magazine declared, "Shopping the farmer's markets and working with her own suppliers, Oakes culls the best of the brimming Bay Area harvest. . . . Local king salmon came atop a woody bed of chanterelle mushrooms, and pancetta-wrapped tuna came with heirloom tomatoes, fennel and fingerling potatoes. This was the kind of purist's food that locates the pulse of each ingredient."

Nancy Oakes didn't attend a culinary school. Instead, she earned her status by apprenticing with several of France's greatest chefs, including Girard Boyer at Taillevent, Guy Savoy, and Joël Robuchon. She then moved to San Francisco, where she studied at the San Francisco Art Institute and paid her rent by working at such high-profile restaurants as Alexis. A few years later, she and a friend created a popular waterfront restaurant, Barnacle. This led to L'Avenue, a 50-seat San Francisco neighborhood bistro. Oakes and restaurant designer/culinary entrepreneur Pat Kuleto formed a partnership and located Boulevard on a San Francisco waterfront site that was one of the few structures to survive the San Francisco earthquake and fire of 1906. The sumptuous Belle Epoch interior features 145 seats.

Oakes, who had been nominated by the James Beard Foundation as the Best Chef in California in 1997, 1998, 1999, and 2000, received this coveted honor in 2001. She is married to Bruce Aidells, the famous sausage-maker.

Awards & Honors

Boulevard Restaurant

2001 James Beard Foundation, Best Chef in California

1998–2003 *Zagat Survey*—San Francisco's Bay Area's Favorite Restaurant

Food & Wine magazine: Best Restaurant San Francisco, 2000; San Francisco's Quintessential Spot, 1999; Best New Chef, 1993

1997 *Wine Spectator:* Top Seven San Francisco Restaurants

Patrick O'Connell

Awards & Honors

The Inn at Little Washington

***** *Mobil Travel Guide*

AAA, 5-Diamonds Award

#1 in *Zagat's Washington, D.C. Restaurant Survey*

1994–2002 *Wine Spectator's* "Grand Award"

2001 Outstanding Chef of the Year

1998 James Beard Foundation, Best Wine List Award

1997 James Beard Foundation, as Best Service Award

1993 James Beard Foundation, Best Chef—Mid-Atlantic

1993 James Beard Foundation, Best Restaurant of the Year

Cigar Aficionado's "Grand Cru" award for restaurant's wine list

Gourmet magazine, "Reader's Top Table" award

Photo by Jan Bartelsman

Patrick O'Connell, a native of Washington, D.C., is a self-taught chef who pioneered a refined, regional American cuisine in the Virginia countryside. He has been referred to as "the Pope of American Haute Cuisine." Selecting The Inn at Little Washington as one of the top ten restaurants in the world, Patricia Wells of *The International Herald Tribune* hails O'Connell as "a rare chef with a sense of near perfect taste, like a musician with perfect pitch."

The Inn at Little Washington was created by Patrick O'Connell and his partner, Reinhardt Lynch, in 1978. It became America's first five-star country house hotel and the first establishment in the *Mobil Travel Guide's* history to receive two five-star awards—for its restaurant and for its accommodations. The Inn also received AAA's highest accolades—two Five-Diamonds awards—and it is rated number one in all categories year after year by the Washington, D.C. *Zagat Restaurant Survey*. The James Beard Foundation named the inn Restaurant of the Year in 1993 and named O'Connell Best Chef in the Mid-Atlantic Region; most recently, it honored him with the prestigious Outstanding Chef Award for 2001. O'Connell was one of the original inductees into "Who's Who of Food and Beverage in America" and is the recipient of an Honorary Doctorate Degree in the Culinary Arts from Johnson & Wales University.

O'Connell is the author of the best-selling cookbook, *The Inn at Little Washington Cookbook, A Consuming Passion*. He has appeared on many television programs, including *Good Morning America*, the *Today Show*, and *Charlie Rose*, and is a frequent guest speaker at The Smithsonian Institution.

Ken Oringer

As with so many chefs, Ken Oringer began his cooking career at the tender age of sixteen, washing dishes in a local restaurant near his home in Paramus, New Jersey. His ambition to become a chef began at an early age. His parents, who allowed him free rein in their kitchen, often took Oringer to Little Italy and Chinatown in nearby New York City, where the young man was totally smitten with the food. After earning a degree in hotel-restaurant management at Bryant College in Rhode Island, he attended the Culinary Institute of America in New York, where he was voted "Most Likely to Succeed" by his classmates in 1989.

Immediately after graduation, Oringer launched his career working alongside David Burke at The River Café in New York City, and soon afterward took a job as pastry chef at the renowned Al Forno in Providence, Rhode Island. He also briefly worked as sous chef under Jean-Georges Vongerichten at Boston's Marquis de Lafayette and was chef/owner of the short-lived Terra, a Mediterranean trattoria in Greenwich, Connecticut, which received three stars from *The New York Times*.

In 1992, Oringer decided to see what was going on in California. He began in San Francisco, where he was appointed chef de cuisine at Silks in San Francisco's deluxe Mandarin Oriental Hotel. It was at Silks that he began to attract attention for his distinctive, Asian-accented style and his bold use of cutting-edge ingredients. *Condé Nast Traveler* magazine named Silks "one of the top restaurants in America," and more raves followed in the *Zagat Survey* and *Gourmet* magazine.

Three years later, Oringer was back on the east coast, where he won similar praise for his Italian cuisine at Tosca in Hingham, Massachusetts. During the year he cooked there, Tosca was anointed as the "Best South Shore Restaurant," and Oringer was the subject of a profile on CNN News.

In 1997, Oringer created Clio, which is part of the elegant Elliot Hotel (in which he has a partnership interest) in Boston. As executive chef and

Awards & Honors

Clio

2002 James Beard Foundation, Nominated for Outstanding Service

2001 James Beard Foundation, Best Chef—Northeast

2001 James Beard Foundation, Outstanding Restaurant Award

1999 *Bon Appétit,* Best of Food & Entertaining, "Food Artisan"

1999 *Nation's Restaurant News,* "50 New Taste Makers"

1998 and 1999 James Beard Foundation, Nomination for Best Chef—Northeast

1997 IACP Julia Child Cookbook Awards Nominee

1997 James Beard Foundation, Nominated for Best Cookbook of the Year

1997 DiRoNA, Distinguished Restaurant of North America

1996 *Nation's Restaurant News* Fine Dining Award

Photo by Michael James O'Brien

1995 *Chocolatier Magazine*, One of the 10 Best Pastry Chefs of the Year

1995 Southern California Restaurant Writers, Restaurant of the Year & Restaurateur of the Year

1994 Los Angeles Culinary Master of the Year, The 1994 Fine Spirit Wine & Food Tasting Exhibition

1990 James Beard Foundation, Who's Who in American Cooking

1990 James Beard Foundation, Best Pastry Chef of the Year

1989 *Food & Wine* magazine, Best New Chefs

*** *The New York Times* for Terra (Greenwich, CT)

Condé Nast Traveler magazine, One of the Top Restaurants in America—Silks (San Francisco)

co-owner, he was again at the helm of his own restaurant. Oringer's inspired, contemporary French-American menu artfully combined schooled technique with an Asian-inspired approach to food. *Gourmet* magazine named Clio "Best Newcomer" in that year's Top Tables issue, and the restaurant continued to receive accolades from dozens of regional and national publications. Nominated twice in 1998 and 1999 for "Best Chef—Northeast by the James Beard Foundation, Oringer finally captured the prize in 2001.

When asked to name the principal cooking influences of his own career, Oringer generously cites David Burke, Jean-Georges Vongerichten, Paris's legendary Joël Robuchon, and Jacques Pépin.

Odessa Piper

"Choosing lovingly grown food within our region is a powerful way to support our local economy and ecology," says Odessa Piper, chef-proprietor of L'Etoile in Madison, Wisconsin. "This is the true mission of sustainable agriculture." Ms. Piper was the 2001 recipient of the James Beard Foundation Award for Best Chef—Midwest. The award was a powerful endorsement of Piper's philosophy of creating menus composed of local ingredients all year round, and achieved through partnerships with a large network of small-scale farms. She divides the year into nine—not four—seasons: early spring, late spring, early summer, high summer, Indian summer, fall, late fall, winter, and late winter. The foods she serves at L'Etoile are taken from each season.

Piper grew up on the New England coast in a large family with many cooking and foraging traditions. After high school, she farmed in Canaan, New Hampshire, with a small group dedicated to sustainable agriculture. In 1969, she moved to Madison, Wisconsin, where she helped open a restaurant called the Ovens of Brittany. During this period, Piper discovered the area's native hickory nuts, morels, and wild plums. She became excited by the possibility of creating menus based on the exceptional quality of local ingredients, and in 1976, she decided to open her L'Etoile.

Piper's regionally reliant cuisine has advanced her menu ideas to a point where she has been invited to participate in a White House dinner, as well as gaining exposure to a wide variety of media including features in *Gourmet*, *Sierra Magazine*, *Bon Appétit*, *Food & Wine*, *Wine Spectator*, *The New York Times*, *The Wall Street Journal*, Wisconsin Public Radio, and NPR. Some highlights of her other TV and radio appearances include "Chefs Afield" for PBS-TV, "Cooking in America with Pierre Franey," and "All About Food with Jean Feraca" for Wisconsin Public Radio. Her recipes have also appeared in *Food Arts*, *Eating Well*, the *New York Times*, the *Chicago Tribune*, the *Wall Street Journal*, *Milwaukee Journal*, *Nation's Restaurant News*, *Fine Cooking*, and *Organic Gardening*. Piper divides her time between cooking, writing, consulting and public speaking. She frequently accompanies her husband, wine importer Terry Theise, on his travels throughout France, Germany and Austria.

Awards & Honors

L'Etoile

1986–present "Favorite" or "Best" restaurant in reader polls in *Madison Magazine, Milwaukee Magazine,* and others

2002 *Nation's Restaurant News* Hall of Fame

2001 *Gourmet* magazine, Favorite 50 Restaurants in the U.S.

2001 James Beard Foundation, Best Chef—Midwest

Photo courtesy Brent Nicastro/ Photographer
1707 Rutledge St.
Madison, WI 53704
608-244-3098

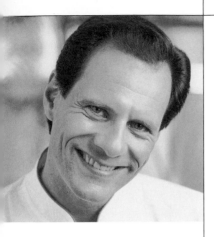

Michael Romano

Awards & Honors

Union Square Cafe

2002 *Where Magazine,* Best Downtown Dining

2002 *Nation's Restaurant News,* Menu Masters Best Independent Operator Menu

1997–2002 *Zagat Survey,* #1 Favorite New York Restaurant

2001 *Food Arts,* Silver Spoon Award

2001 James Beard Foundation, Best Chef in New York City

2001 *Wine Spectator,* Best of Award of Excellence

2000 ***Forbes Magazine*

2000 James Beard Foundation, Who's Who of Food & Beverage

1988–2000 *Wine Spectator,* Award of Excellence

1999 James Beard Foundation, Outstanding Wine Service Award

1999 *Gourmet* magazine, Top for Wine

For the past six years, Union Square Cafe has been voted the "Number One, Most Popular Restaurant" in the New York City *Zagat Survey*—a record. The restaurant's spectacular rise to this coveted position has come about during the tenure of its chef, Michael Romano, who has led the restaurant to its current eminence since 1988. In partnership with Danny Meyer, who created Union Square Cafe, Romano has gone on to help lay the culinary foundations for two more must-dine-at Manhattan restaurants: Tabla, which marries American cuisine with the spices of India, and Blue Smoke, featuring genuine pit barbecue and home-style food in New York City.

Romano's first culinary job was at New York's popular Serendipity restaurant in 1971. Without formal training, his potential was spotted early on, and he was quickly promoted from frozen-drink man to evening line cook. The impressed Serendipity owners introduced the talented young cook to the legendary James Beard, who advised and inspired him to attend New York City Technical College. After a semester at a hotel school in Bournemouth, England, he graduated in 1974.

His first job was a *stage* at the illustrious Hotel Bristol in Paris, which was quickly followed by a position at the Hotel Pierre in New York. Then, in 1976, Romano came under the tutelage of France's renowned Michel Guérard, first in the kitchen of Regine's private club in Paris, where Guérard was Culinary Director, and later at the opening of Regine's in New York. He returned to France, this time to Eugenie-les Bains, Guérard's three-star flagship restaurant and spa in the southwest, where he was *commis poissonier* and *saucier*. While still under the auspices of Guérard, he was engaged as personal chef to Swiss entrepreneur Henri Lavanchy. During this period he also completed another *stage* at the two-star Capon Fin restaurant in Bordeaux.

Michael Romano continued to gain valuable experience as Chef de Cuisine at Max Kehl's two-star Chez Max in Zurich. Adding gala events to his resume, he also cooked aboard the Orient Express, acted as chef for a dinner for 100 at London's luxe Dorchester Hotel, and was part of a winning team that took first prize in the hors d'oeuvre category during a 15-country competition held in Tokyo.

In 1984, an extraordinary opportunity urged Romano to New York. He was offered the position as Chef de Cuisine at New York's La Caravelle restaurant—then in its twenty-fifth year. He was only the third chef in the venerable restaurant's history, and the first American to hold the position. Under his direction La Caravelle earned a second star from *The New York Times* during his four-year tenure.

In 1988, Danny Meyer invited Romano to become chef at Union Square Cafe, and just six months after his arrival, *The New York Times* elevated it to three stars. Five years later, Romano and Meyer became partners. In addition to their three restaurants, they have collaborated on two successful cookbooks: *The Union Square Cafe Cookbook* (HarperCollins; Fall of 1994, and winner of an IACP Julia Child Cookbook Award) and *Second Helpings* (HarperCollins; 2001).

Throughout his career, Romano has often been honored by his industry. In 2001, after seven nominations, he received the James Beard Foundation's Best Chef in New York City award. *Food & Wine* magazine cited him as one of the Top Ten Chefs in the U.S.A, and in 2000, he was inducted into the James Beard Foundation's Who's Who of Food & Beverage in America. In 1997, he launched the weekly column "The Chef" in *The New York Times'* "Dining In/Dining Out" section, with a series of eight articles, and was profiled in *Mastery*, a recently published book featuring interviews with "30 Remarkable People."

1999–2002 *Where Magazine,* Best Service

1999 *** *The New York Times,* September 1, 1999

1997 James Beard Foundation, Outstanding Restaurant Award

1996 ***½ *Passport to New York Restaurants*

1995 *** *New York Newsday,* February 17, 1995

1995 **** *Daily News,* November 10, 1995

1996–1999 *Gourmet* magazine, America's Top Tables

1994 IACP Julia Child Cookbook Award

1994 *Restaurants and Institutions'* Ivy Award

1993 *Condé Nast Traveler,* Top 50 American Restaurants

1992–1996 *Travel Holiday,* Good Value Dining Award

1992–1996 Distinguished Restaurants of North America Award

1992 James Beard Foundation, Outstanding Service Award

1992 *Food & Wine* magazine, Top 25 Restaurants in America

1992 *Nation's Restaurant News* Fine Dining Hall of Fame

1991 *Food & Wine* magazine, America's Top 10 Chefs

1989 *** *The New York Times,* May 12, 1989

Nancy Silverton and Mark Peel

Nancy Silverton is pastry chef and co-owner of Campanile restaurant and baker and owner of La Brea Bakery of Los Angeles. Mark Peel is executive chef and co-owner of Campanile restaurant. Silverton and Peel opened Campanile restaurant in 1989, where it quickly established itself as one of the great dining experiences in Southern California. Its reputation has continued to soar ever since.

Silverton was born and raised in Los Angeles, California. Nancy was 18 years old and studying liberal arts at California State University, Sonoma, when she began working as a vegetarian cook in her dormitory kitchen. After apprenticing at a small northern California restaurant, she attended the Cordon Bleu in London. She then returned to Los Angeles, where she was employed as an assistant pastry chef at Michael's restaurant in Santa Monica.

The turning point in her career occurred after completing a series of pastry courses at the Ecole Le Notre in Plaiser, France. Soon after, Silverton was appointed head pastry chef at Wolfgang Puck's Spago restaurant, where she was responsible for developing the highly acclaimed desserts.

In 1985, she and her husband, Mark Peel, moved to Manhattan and spent six months revamping Maxwell's Plum. Returning to Los Angeles, Nancy opened La Brea Bakery in January 1989; next door, Campanile opened its doors the following June.

Nancy is the author of four cookbooks: *Desserts* (Harper & Row), *Nancy Silverton's Breads from the La Brea Bakery* (Villard Books), *Nancy Silverton's Pastries from the La Brea Bakery* (Villard Books), and *Nancy Silverton's Sandwich Book* (Knopf). She has also co-authored two

Awards & Honors

NANCY SILVERTON
Campanile and La Brea Bakery

2002   James Beard Foundation, Nominated for Outstanding Service

2001   James Beard Foundation, Outstanding Restaurant Award

1999   *Bon Appétit,* Best of Food & Entertaining, Food Artisan

1999   *Nation's Restaurant News,* 50 New Taste Makers

1997   IACP Julia Child Cookbook Awards Nominee

1997   James Beard Foundation, Nominated for Best Cookbook of the Year

1997   DiRoNA, Distinguished Restaurant of North America

1996   *Nation's Restaurant News* Fine Dining Award

1995   *Chocolatier Magazine,* One of the 10 Best Pastry Chefs of the Year

1995   Southern California Restaurant Writers, Restaurant of the Year & Restauranteur of the Year

cookbooks with Mark: *Mark Peel and Nancy Silverton at Home*; *Two Chefs Cook for Family and Friends* (Warner Books) and *The Food of Campanile* (Villard Books). Nancy and Mark have three children: Vanessa, Benjamin, and Oliver.

Mark Peel was born and raised in both Southern and Northern California. By the time he was out of high school, Mark had worked in a series of kitchen jobs, which including a stint as a fry cook at Cindy's, a coffee shop that serviced a 24-hour freeway truckstop in the San Gabriel Valley. He majored in history at the University of California at Santa Barbara before transferring to the hotel and restaurant department at California Polytechnic University of Pomona. While still in college he landed a job peeling vegetables for Chef Wolfgang Puck at Ma Maison restaurant. As part of Ma Maison's informal apprenticeship program, he was sent to work at two French three-star restaurants, La Tour d'Argent and Moulin de Mougins. Mark was sous chef at Michael's restaurant in Santa Monica when he met his future wife, pastry chef Nancy Silverton.

Before working for three and a half years as head chef under Wolfgang Puck at Spago, he spent a year working at the influential Chez Panisse in Berkeley, California. In 1985, he and Silverton put in six months revamping Maxwell's Plum in New York. In June of 1989, the couple opened Campanile restaurant.

Campanile has an interesting history. It was originally built in 1929 by Hollywood legend Charlie Chaplin. He intended to create his own office space, but before it was completed, he lost the building in a divorce settlement with his first wife, Lita Grey. In the late 1980s, architect Josh Sweitzer adapted the building for Mark Peel and Nancy Silverton and wine buyer, Manfred Kranki, for what was to become a bakery and a restaurant.

La Brea Bakery and Campanile have received numerous awards, nominations, and honors including the James Beard Outstanding Restaurant Award, Distinguished Restaurant of North America, *Nation's Restaurant News* of North America, Los Angeles Culinary Master of the Year, and nominated for James Beard Outstanding Wine Service and James Beard Best California Chef. Mark has a new restaurant in Los Angeles, called Jar, a modern chop house that he opened with Suzanne Tracht.

1994   Los Angeles Culinary Master of the Year, The 1994 Fine Spirit Wine & Food Tasting Exhibition

1990   James Beard Foundation, Who's Who in American Cooking

1990   James Beard Foundation, Best Pastry Chef of the Year

1989   *Food & Wine* magazine, Best New Chefs

Awards & Honors

MARK PEEL

2002   James Beard Foundation, Nominated for Best American Chef, California

2002   James Beard Foundation, Nominated for Outstanding Service

2001   James Beard Foundation, Outstanding Restaurant Award

2001   James Beard Foundation, Nominated for Best American Chef, California

1997   DiRoNA, Distinguished Restaurant of North America

1996   *Nation's Restaurant News* Fine Dining Award

1996   James Beard Foundation, Nominated for Best American Chef, California

1995   Southern California Restaurant Writers, Restaurateur of the Year & Restaurant of the Year

1995   James Beard Foundation, Nominated for Best American Chef, California

1990   James Beard Foundation, Nominated for Best American Chef, California

1989   *Food & Wine* magazine, Best New Chefs

Awards & Honors

Highlands Bar & Grill

2001 *Gourmet* magazine, selected fifth best restaurant in the nation

2001 James Beard Foundation, Best Chef—Southeast

2001 *Wine Spectator* "Award of Excellence," Highlands and Bottega

1991–1999, *Birmingham Magazine*—voted Birmingham's Best Restaurant

1993 Inducted as member of Leadership Birmingham

1992 *Nation's Restaurant News,* Voted into the Fine Dining Hall of Fame

Food & Wine magazine, Top 25 Hot New American Chefs

A James Beard Foundation Rising Star of American Cuisine

A James Beard Foundation Great Regional Chef

Esquire magazine Best Regional Restaurant

SOS Great Chefs of America

Frank Stitt's fondness for southern ingredients comes from his roots in rural Alabama (he was born in Cullman, Alabama). Yet his culinary journey began in San Francisco, where he studied philosophy at the University of California at Berkeley and came under the influence of Alice Waters. In Europe, Simone Beck, Richard Olney, and wine authority Stephen Spurrier became mentors. Stitt's travels took him throughout the French countryside, working in vineyards in Provence as well as Burgundy, and finally back to Birmingham and to the foods and traditions that continue to be so much a part of his vision. His first restaurant, the award-winning Highlands Bar & Grill, opened in 1982 and gave him a national reputation. Here, he combined French technique and the seasonal flavors of "both souths"—France and the United States. Highlands was named "Best Regional Restaurant" by *Esquire* magazine. But it's the locals who say it best: Highlands has been voted Birmingham's best restaurant every year since 1991.

Stitt's restlessness led to trips in Italy, Greece, and Spain. He didn't want to muddle those influences with the essentially French theme at Highlands. Instead he opened Bottega and Café Bottega. The more formal Bottega is a showcase for the foods of Italy and the Mediterranean, including simple Venetian fish dishes and Tuscan roasts as well as spices and regional complexities of North Africa, Andalusia, and the Mediterranean basin. Café Bottega is conceived along the same lines as a busy trattoria. It has an open kitchen and a wood-fired brick oven for pizzas, roast pork loin with polenta, and a seasonally changing menu.

In May 2000, Frank Stitt increased his restaurant group to include Chez Fonfon, a casual drop-in place like the familiar and comfortable corner cafés so beloved in Paris, Lyons, or Bandol. Here the focus is on "small" foods and drinks. The café atmosphere was created with turn-of-the-century furnishings, a boule court, and a wine barrel imported from Provence.

In between managing and cooking in his restaurants, Frank Stitt is still a restless traveler, always on the lookout for new inspiration. In 1999, he took a fabulous culinary tour of France, spending time in the kitchen of the legendary Taillevent and harvesting olives in Greece. He is frequently asked to guest chef or to speak for numerous culinary events, including Napa Valley Wine Auction, AIWF, Bacchus Society, Symposium on American Cuisine, IWFS, Callaway Gardens, The Cloister, and James Beard House.

Stitt has been a Consulting Editor to *Saveur* magazine since 1994. Frequent feature articles on Stitt's work and all three restaurants have appeared in *Gourmet, Metropolitan Home, Art Culinaire, Bon Appétit, Food & Wine, Travel and Leisure, Southern Living, Southern Accents, Wine Spectator, Playboy, Esquire, Harper's Bazaar, Ladies' Home Journal, McCall's, Woman's Day, Restaurant Business, The New York Times, USA Today,* Delta Airlines' *Sky Magazine,* and Cooking.com.

Named one of the *Independent Restaurant* magazine's 25 Shining Stars

Board of Directors: Chef's Collaborative

Board of Directors: Southern Foodways Alliance

Statewide Chair: Share Our Strength

Food Chair: "Magic Moments" Wine Auction, an annual fund-raiser to benefit terminally ill children

Food Chair: "An Event in Three Acts," an annual fund-raiser for Birmingham AIDS Outreach

Featured chef on the Discovery Channel's "Great Chefs, Great Cities" television series

Featured on the Food Network's "Best of . . ." series

Charlie Trotter

Charlie Trotter started cooking professionally in 1982 after graduating with a degree in political science from the University of Wisconsin. At that time he embarked on an intense four-year period of work, study, and travel, working and studying with Norman Van Aiken, Bradley Ogden, and Gordon Sinclair. He lived in Chicago, San Francisco, Florida, and Europe, "reading every cookbook I could get my hands on, working like a maniac, and eating out incessantly."

Chef Trotter's cuisine at his eponymously named Chicago-based restaurant originates from the finest foodstuffs available. Utilizing a network of more than ninety purveyors who provide him with the freshest ingredients, Trotter is inspired to create flavorful masterpieces. From the naturally raised meat and line-caught seafood to the organic produce, every component of each dish is the purest available. Indiana bobwhite quail, petite greens from Farmer Jones, heirloom tomatoes from Illinois, North Dakota buffalo, and Hawaiian gindai are just a few of the products that arrive each day and from which Chef Trotter crafts his daily menus. Harvey Steiman observes in the *Wine Spectator* that "Trotter regards recipes the way jazz musicians see their musical scores—as frameworks for improvisation. The results follow a discipline, but they spring from the moment, not a carefully plotted script."

Charlie Trotter's has established itself as one of the finest restaurants in the world. The restaurant is recognized by a variety of prestigious national and international institutions including Relais & Chateaux: Relais Gourmand; *Mobil Travel Guide:* Five Stars; AAA: Five Diamonds; Traditions & Qualité; The James Beard Foundation: Who's Who of Food and Beverage in America; and the Award for Outstanding Wine Service. The restaurant has received the Grand Award from *Wine Spectator*, which also recently named Charlie Trotter's as Best Restaurant in the United States (2000).

Charlie Trotter has managed to keep busy, producing a stunning series of lavishly photographed and meticulously detailed cookbooks, based mainly on the dishes he serves at the restaurant, including *Charlie Trotter's* (Ten Speed Press, 1994), *Charlie Trotter's Vegetables* (Ten Speed Press, 1996), *Charlie Trotter's Seafood* (Ten Speed Press, 1997), *Charlie Trotter's Desserts* (Ten Speed Press, 1998), *Charlie Trotter's Meat and Game* (Ten Speed Press, 2001), *The Kitchen Sessions with Charlie Trotter* (Ten Speed Press, 1999), *Cooking with Patrick Clark: A Tribute to the Man and His Cuisine* by Charlie Trotter and Friends (Ten Speed Press, 1999), *Charlie Trotter Cooks at Home* (Ten Speed Press, 2000), and *Gourmet Cooking for Dummies* (Hungry Minds/John Wiley & Sons, 1997).

Trotter spends his "spare" time performing cooking demonstrations, giving speeches, and consulting. He dedicates as much time as possible to charitable organizations. His efforts include providing over 300 donations to charity auctions each year; organizing the American Cancer Society's Vinnaffair, which raised over one million dollars in two years; donating proceeds from the restaurant's tenth anniversary to The Mercy Home for Boys and Girls; spear-heading a cookbook dedicated to the late chef Patrick Clark; and creating the Charlie Trotter's Culinary Education Foundation. Chef Trotter is also a Board of Trustee member of the James Beard Foundation and serves on the Kennedy-King College Culinary Advisory Board.

Chicago Tribune:

Four stars (highest rating)

The James Beard Foundation:

Best Food Photography, *Charlie Trotter's Meat & Game*, 2002

Avero Outstanding Service Award, 2002

Outstanding Restaurant, 2000

Best National Television Cooking Show for "The Kitchen Sessions, with Charlie Trotter," 2000

Outstanding Chef Award, 1999

Who's Who in Food & Beverage Award, 1996

Outstanding Wine Service, 1993

Best Chef, Midwest, 1992

Nation's Restaurant News:

50 Power Players 2000

Fine Dining Hall of Fame (elected by peers), 1991

Crain's Chicago Business:

Four Forks (highest rating)

Frederick Wildman & Sons:

Moreau Award for Excellence in the Culinary Arts

Restaurants and Institutions:

Fine Dining Ivy Award (elected by peers), 1990

Snacks, First Courses, and Sandwiches

SERVES 4 TO 6

I would hate to have to choose between Spanish ham, American country ham, or Italian hams like prosciutto, but if I had to, I'd pick the Spanish hams produced from its black-footed pigs who feed upon acorns: jamon jabugo. If you can't find that or the Spanish ser-rano, use prosciutto. This dish makes a wonderful snack or light first course.

Grilled Green Beans Wrapped in Serrano Ham with Toasted Almond Dressing and Manchego Cheese

1 pound	thin French green beans (haricots verts)
	salt and freshly ground pepper
12 slices	serrano ham or prosciutto, cut into paper-thin slices
1/2 pound	tango lettuce or mixed lettuces
	For the dressing
1/2 cup	whole natural almonds (skins on)
2 tablespoons	minced fresh shallots
1	lemon, juiced
2 tablespoons	white balsamic vinegar
1 tablespoon	champagne vinegar
	salt and freshly ground pepper
1 cup	extra virgin olive oil
1 tablespoon	chopped fresh tarragon leaves
1 tablespoon	chopped fresh parsley leaves
1 teaspoon	chopped fresh thyme leaves
1/3 cup	diced (1/4-inch) Manchego cheese

Line up the beans and cut off both ends, making even lengths about 3 inches long. Boil in a large pot of heavily salted boiling water for 3 minutes, or until the beans are crisp-tender. Drain and refresh in a bowl of ice water; drain and pat dry.

Arrange the beans in 12 equal piles. Season them with salt and pepper. Wrap each pile in a slice of the ham.

One of my key restaurant peeves [is] undercooked vegetables. You have to cook vegetables in a lot of boiling salted water, in enough water so that the water comes back to the boil very quickly after the vegetables have been added.

—NANCY OAKES

Preheat the oven to 325°F.

Spread out the almonds on a baking sheet and toast in the oven, stirring them up once, until fragrant and browned, 8 to 12 minutes. Let cool, then coarsely chop.

To make the dressing, mix the shallots, lemon juice, and white balsamic and champagne vinegars in a medium bowl with a pinch each of salt and pepper. Gradually whisk in the olive oil. Add the herbs, chopped almonds, and Manchego cheese.

Grill or broil the wrapped beans, under medium heat, turning, for 6 to 8 minutes, until the beans are tender and the ham is lightly browned.

To serve, crisscross 2 bean bundles on each plate. Dress the lettuce with 3 tablespoons of the dressing and arrange in equal piles on each plate. Spoon the remaining dressing over the bean bundles and around the plates.

Nancy Oakes's Grilled Green Beans Wrapped in Serrano Ham.

JEREMIAH TALKS ABOUT

Odessa Piper L'Etoile, Madison, Wisconsin

IN A BRIEF DESCRIPTION OF A PERSON, ALMOST ANYTHING SOUNDS LIKE A SIMPLIFICATION. But with Odessa Piper, nothing is more telling than her response as I was bemoaning America's horror at blemishes on fruit and vegetables: "The little bug bites tell me the fruit has been pre-approved." Only Odessa would see the insect world as her partner and not an enemy, and then relate it to how she buys food, cooks it, and creates the feeling and experience of her restaurant L'Etoile.

On the wall of the restaurant dining room is a map of all her hundreds of farm suppliers around Wisconsin. It is a celebration of how she, with her usual perfect clarity, sees sustainability: when all relations prosper, and when everyone does well—the supplier, the restaurant, and the person buying the food.

As she was talking about the kind of farming (both land and ocean) that will give us all the ingredients we want without destroying their environment and which would still provide a good living for all, I could not help thinking that both she and her restaurant L'Etoile are a metaphor for—or even a living example of—what she believes. The restaurant, she said, is modeled after an organic garden, choosing patient growth over short-term gains.

After that conversation and another about "baby pictures" (working with her suppliers from the first moment of the development of an ingredient through all its stages to its optimum moment, flavor, and use), we set off for Janie Crawford's farm outside of Madison to pick out a free-range leg of lamb.

I couldn't wait to cook the meat, but first we filled huge *gougères* (cheese puffs), still warm from the oven, with a salad of hazelnuts and perfect greens picked that morning. Then we cut slices from a leg of lamb and pounded them out to form a layer in which we rolled up spinach wilted with mint and mixed with some feta cheese. The spinach was from the hoop houses of Farmer Jones, a few hours away in Huron, Ohio; the mint was from the garden, and the feta from an organic dairy down the road. The flavor of the lamb was clear, precise, and had none of the heavy flavors of feedlot commercial meat. In fact, everything we cooked was a celebration of the organic and "natural" ingredients increasingly available around America.

But nothing brought out more of Odessa's "mmmmmm, mmmmm," loudly murmured, than the really fresh filbert nut strudel baked in its buttery phyllo dough, served warm with a great big dollop of luscious organic cream and pure maple syrup. As I wiped a bit of buttery strudel from my chin, the message from Madison, Wisconsin, was clear: buy what the farmer would eat himself, cook it simply, and serve it with love.

ODESSA PIPER

SERVES 4 TO 6

Gougères and Winter Green Salad with Apples and Cheese

Odessa serves these cheese puffs with a salad of winter greens, but gougères are also ideal to offer for a snack with drinks. They can be filled with leftovers and used to make large finger sandwiches as well.

Blended with mashed potatoes, this paste makes gnocchi. When mixed with fish or chicken puree, the same paste becomes a mousse or quenelles. And when sweetened (and the cheese omitted), it makes the puffs for éclairs.

Odessa makes sure the eggs are warm by putting them in a couple of consecutive baths of warm water. She uses Stravicchio cheese, but you can substitute grated imported Swiss, such as Gruyère or Emmenthaler or a mixture of Swiss and grated Parmigiano-Reggiano.

1 recipe	Gougères (recipe follows)
4 cups	mixed baby lettuces, herbs, and greens, loosely packed
1	large shallot, peeled, minced, and crushed to a paste
3 tablespoons	white wine vinegar
	salt and freshly ground pepper
5 tablespoons	light extra virgin olive oil
1 tablespoon	fresh walnut oil
1/4 cup	finely chopped toasted, skinned hazelnuts
2	apples, preferably orange Cox pippin, peeled, cored, quartered, very thinly sliced
1/4 pound	Pleasant Ridge Reserve Wisconsin Beaufort-style cheese, rind removed, or Gruyère or Emmenthaler

Make the Gougères as described in the recipe that follows and set aside. Rinse and dry the greens for the salad.

To make the salad dressing, mix the shallot, the vinegar, and salt and pepper in a bowl. Whisk in the olive and walnut oils. Mix in the chopped hazelnuts and sliced apple.

Put the mixed greens in a bowl and pour on the dressing. Toss gently but completely. Place the dressed salad into the gougères, letting some slip out onto the plate. Slice the cheese with a cheese slicer or vegetable peeler over the top of the salad and onto the plate. Dust with a grinding of pepper and serve.

Gougères

1 cup	water
6 tablespoons	unsalted butter, plus 2 tablespoons for buttering sheets
1 teaspoon	salt
1 cup	all-purpose flour, sifted
	freshly ground white pepper
4	large eggs
1³/₄ cups	shredded Stravicchio cheese or Gruyère

Crisp on the outside and soft within, this Burgundian specialty can be made in a large ring or as here, in small puffs, perfect to serve as hot hors d'oeuvres or as an accompaniment to a salad.

Preheat the oven to 425°F.

Boil the water in a 2-quart saucepan with the 6 tablespoons butter and the salt. Remove from the heat and beat in the flour all at once with a wooden spoon. Beat the mixture vigorously until the paste is smooth and pulls away from the pan, or "rounds itself." Add a few grinds of the white pepper.

Either by hand or in a mixer, beat in the eggs one at a time until fully incorporated. Then mix in the cheese. Stop beating when the batter is stiff.

Butter a baking sheet and put the paste into a pastry bag fitted with a ³/₄-inch round tube tip. Squeeze the paste onto the baking sheets in mounds 2¹/₂ inches in diameter and 1 inch high in the center. Alternatively, the paste can be dropped from a spoon, but the shapes will not be as neat. Make sure the mounds are at least 2 inches apart.

Bake for 5 minutes. Reduce the oven temperature to 350°F and cook for another 20 minutes. Set the puffs on the door of the turned-off oven for 15 minutes to dry out. Cut off the very top of the puffs and scoop out any damp interior pastry. (The tops are for snacks.)

Tip: Because gougères "take very well to reheating," you can make these the day before.

Odessa Piper's Gougères and Winter Green Salad with Apples and Cheese.

Potato Tartiflette

SERVES 4

1 clove	garlic, peeled, cut in half
1 tablespoon	unsalted butter, at room temperature
1/2 pound	smoked bacon, cut in 1/4-inch dice
1	small onion, peeled, finely chopped
1 pound	fingerling potatoes, boiled until almost done, peeled, sliced 1/4 inch thick
	salt and freshly ground pepper
1/2 pound	Reblochon cheese, crust removed, sliced 1/8 inch thick
4 sprigs	fresh thyme

Jean-Marie describes this dish as *cuisine familiale,* or family cooking, from the Savoy, *alpes* region of Southwestern France. It is a fast dish to do, can be prepared in advance up to the final heating, and is perfect, he says, for *après-ski.*

You will need four individual gratin dishes or one large one.

Preheat the oven to 400°F.

Rub the insides of the gratin dishes thoroughly with the cut ends of the garlic and then with the butter.

Cook the bacon in a large frying pan over medium heat until the fat starts to render out. Then add the onion and the sliced potatoes. Stir all the ingredients together gently and cook for another 5 minutes. Season with salt and pepper.

Fill the gratin dishes equally with the potato and bacon mixture. Cover them with the slices of Reblochon.

Bake in the oven for 30 minutes. Serve immediately, with ground pepper on top and a sprig of fresh thyme stuck into each dish for garnish.

Jean-Marie Lacroix's Potato Tartiflette.

Fava Bean "à la Croque"

JEAN-MARIE LACROIX

| 3 pounds | young fava beans in their pods |
| 2 tablespoons | fleur de sel sea salt |

SERVES 4 TO 6

Take the fava beans out of their pods and peel off their skins. Discard the pods and skins.

Chop the favas coarsely and divide equally among 16 Chinese spoons. Sprinkle with the sea salt, put on a tray, and serve.

This is a great party snack. It may not sound like much when reading the recipe, but the tastes and presentation are wonderful. Once you have double-peeled the favas, that is.

For serving, you will need 16 Chinese spoons, or keep cleaning and re-using 8 of them. Garnish the tray with herb flowers or nasturtiums.

Jean-Marie Lacroix's Fava Bean "à la Croque."

Snacks, First Courses, and Sandwiches

Alain Ducasse Alain Ducasse at the Essex House, New York

YOU CAN TELL A LOT ABOUT A PERSON WHEN THEY ARE COOKING, but when the chef is Alain Ducasse, preconceptions fly out the window. You might expect that the world's most famous chef—who has restaurants in several countries and a travel schedule that would devastate any secretary of state—would have only minutes to spare for our cooking session together. But the day I cooked with Ducasse in New York, there was not a hint of jet lag—or of trying to shave minutes off the real time needed for cooking a dish perfectly just so that he could get on with the rest of his schedule.

Ducasse was organized, calm, and patience personified. The love he showed for his *steak au poivre,* refusing to rush the simple and almost forgotten sauce; the tenderness with which he assembled his BLT; the sense of humor that he showed with his "chocolate pizza" (page 152); and the time he took to cut it up himself for everyone in the room to have a taste showed me that this is a man with heart.

Now, chocolate pizza may sound a bit over the top, but once you have entered the unique universe of Alain Ducasse, you realize that nothing in it is. *Au contraire,* all the food is disciplined in the restraint imposed by using no more than three or four main ingredients per recipe. And each dish is passionate, luxuriously simple, and designed to be out of this world. Less-than-perfect cooking has nowhere to hide from the wonderful directness and simplicity of his food. Many times in history great men have believed that less is definitely more, and Alain is no exception to that rule.

Spoon's Open-Face BLT

24 strips	bacon
6	baby romaine or limestone lettuce hearts
4 tablespoons	extra virgin olive oil
1 tablespoon	sherry vinegar
	sea salt and freshly ground pepper
4 thick slices	country bread, cut 3/4 inch thick
1 clove	garlic, peeled, cut in half
3 tablespoons	Spoon's Pesto (recipe follows)
3 tablespoons	Three-Tomato Marmalade (recipe follows) or tomato preserves
4 tablespoons	black olive tapenade (homemade or purchased)
24	small Baked Tomatoes Confit (page 145)

Preheat the oven to 350°F.

Arrange the bacon strips on a baking sheet and bake until just crisp, about 12 minutes. Drain on paper towels. Finely chop 4 of the bacon slices; keep the others warm.

Wash and spin-dry the lettuce hearts. Cut them in half lengthwise. Put the lettuce in a bowl and dress in the olive oil and sherry vinegar. Season with salt and pepper.

Grill or toast the bread slices on one side. Rub the toasted side with garlic. Alternately spread pesto, tomato marmalade, and tapenade on the slices of bread, creating 3 distinct layers of each on all the slices. Arrange the lettuce hearts on the bread, add the tomatoes confit, and then the sliced bacon. Shower with the chopped bacon, drizzle with more olive oil, and sprinkle with salt and pepper. Serve whole with a knife and fork.

ALAIN DUCASSE

SERVES 4

Since I adore sandwiches—they are a perfect food—and clubs, open-face sandwiches, and BLTs are my favorites, I could not resist asking Alain Ducasse to make this sandwich when we cooked together in New York for television. He was surprised and pleased.

This version is as easy as any BLT, except for the tomato marmalade (page 38). I suggest you keep some of it in a jar in your refrigerator at all times, using it frequently so that it stays fresh. Or use a puree of oven-dried ones you do yourself (see my oven-cooked tomatoes on page 146).

If you don't have baby romaine or limestone lettuce, use the smallest inner leaves of regular lettuce heads.

Spoon's Pesto

3 cloves	garlic, peeled, smashed
1/2 teaspoon	salt
3¹/₂ tablespoons	olive oil
1 bunch	basil, stemmed
¹/₄ cup	pine nuts, lightly toasted, crushed
2 tablespoons	freshly grated Parmesan cheese
1/2 teaspoon	freshly ground black pepper

Put the garlic, salt, and olive oil in a mortar or small bowl in which you can crush it. Use a pestle or spoon to crush it to a puree. Add the basil leaves and continue to work into a puree. Add the crushed pine nuts, Parmesan cheese, and pepper and work another minute until smooth.

Three-Tomato Marmalade

MAKES ABOUT 2 CUPS

1 tablespoon	olive oil
1 cup	chopped, seeded ripe red tomatoes (about 3)
1 cup	fresh sun-dried tomatoes in olive oil
1	Baked Tomato Confit (page 145)

Heat the olive oil in a 10-inch frying pan until just before smoking. Add the chopped fresh tomatoes and cook for 30 seconds, or just until all the water is evaporated. Remove from the heat and let cool.

Chop the sun-dried and oven-dried tomatoes to a coarse puree. Mix with the cooked fresh tomatoes.

Pizza with Wild Boletus Mushrooms and Virginia Ham

JEREMIAH TOWER

SERVES 4 TO 6

4 tablespoons	extra virgin olive oil
4 sprigs	fresh thyme, very coarsely chopped
4 cloves	garlic, peeled, coarsely chopped
2	large fresh boletus mushrooms (porcini or cèpes)
1 recipe	Pizza Dough (page 203)
	salt and freshly ground pepper
8 slices	Virginia ham or prosciutto, sliced paper-thin, cut into 4-inch squares each

Mix 2 tablespoons of the olive oil with the thyme and garlic and rub all over the mushrooms. Let them marinate for 2 hours. Wipe off and reserve the thyme, garlic, and marinade oil. Slice the mushrooms 1/8 inch thick.

Preheat the oven to 300°F.

Place the marinated mushroom slices on a baking sheet. Pour the reserved marinade oil over them and sprinkle with the reserved thyme and garlic. Bake for 10 minutes; remove and let cool. Wipe off and discard the thyme and garlic. Save any juices in the pan.

Raise the oven temperature to 500°F.

Roll out the dough to a 15-inch round. Brush the dough with the remaining olive oil and cover with the mushroom slices in a single layer. Drizzle on any reserved juices. Season with salt and pepper.

Bake the pizza for 7 to 8 minutes, or until the dough is cooked through. Remove from the oven and cover with the slices of ham. Grind a generous amount of pepper over the ham and serve immediately.

When we filmed *America's Best Chefs Cook with Jeremiah Tower* in Patrick O'Connell's Inn at Little Washington, I could not keep my hands off the local boletus mushrooms and Virginia ham from down the road in Culpepper, Virginia. If you don't have fresh boletus, use portobello from the super-market prepared the same way, cooking them 10 minutes longer in the oven before putting them on the pizza. I garnished this pizza with fresh thyme flowers, but that was in the spring.

Tip: Make the pizza dough a day ahead.

PHILIPPE BOULOT

Dungeness Crab Club Sandwich

MAKES 4 SANDWICHES

I have never met any kind of club sandwich I didn't like, and this version is a dream. Aside from the fabulous crab, crisp fresh fennel and applewood-smoked bacon make this particularly delicious.

3	egg yolks ($1/4$ cup)
2 tablespoons	freshly squeezed lemon juice
1 tablespoon	Chinese chili-garlic paste
1 tablespoon	Dijon mustard
	salt
$3/4$ cup	pure olive oil
10 ounces	fresh Dungeness crab meat
1	fennel bulb, peeled of outer layer, cut in $1/8$-inch dice
2	celery ribs, peeled, cut in $1/8$-inch dice
1	small red onion, cut in $1/8$-inch dice
8 slices	applewood-smoked bacon
12 slices	brioche sandwich loaf, sliced $1/4$ inch thick
4 leaves	butter lettuce, washed, spin-dried
2	small ripe tomatoes, sliced $1/8$ inch thick (12 slices)
	freshly ground pepper

Put the egg yolks, lemon juice, chili-garlic paste, mustard, and a pinch of salt in a bowl. Whisk or beat with an electric mixer for 2 minutes. Slowly whisk in the olive oil until the mayonnaise thickens.

Some ingredients for Philippe Boulot's Dungeness Crab Sandwich.

The finished dish.

Pick over the crab meat and remove any shell or bits of cartilage. Add the crab, fennel, celery, and red onion to the mayonnaise. Fold them in very gently.

Cook the bacon in a frying pan or under the broiler for 3 to 5 minutes on each side, until just crisp. Drain the bacon on paper towels and keep warm. Toast the slices of brioche.

To assemble the sandwich, put a lettuce leaf on 4 of the toasts. Arrange 3 slices of tomato on top of each lettuce leaf and season with salt and pepper. Then put the bacon on top of the tomatoes. Divide the crab among 4 slices of toast and put them, crab side up, on top of the bacon and tomato. Top with the other 4 slices of brioche toast, cut into quarters, and serve.

JEAN-MARIE LACROIX

Cheese Fondue on Toast

SERVES 4

Jean-Marie used Comté cheese when we cooked in Philadelphia, but you can use aged Gruyère. This is a perfect open-faced sandwich snack, which takes 15 minutes to prepare. A welcome added garnish for the plates would be herb flowers or shredded nasturtiums.

4 slices	brioche or Challah bread, cut 1/2 inch thick
1/4 cup	kirsch
2 tablespoons	heavy cream
1/2 pound	Gruyère or Comté cheese, grated
2 bunches	garden cress
1/4 cup	mixed fresh herb leaves (basil, tarragon, chervil, Italian parsley)
2 tablespoons	extra virgin olive oil
1 teaspoon	champagne vinegar
	salt and freshly ground pepper

Preheat the oven to 400°F.

Sprinkle the brioche slices equally with the kirsch. Drizzle the cream over them. Then cover the slices with a 2-inch-thick layer of the grated cheese.

Place the slices on a baking sheet and bake them in the oven for 4 minutes, or until the cheese is completely melted.

Dress the cress and herb leaves with the oil, vinegar, and salt and pepper. Serve the salad immediately at the side of the toasts.

Salads and Soups

SERVES 4

At the Highlands Bar & Grill, Frank Stitt occasionally serves this salad with roasted beets, sometimes including curly endive, bibb lettuce and watercress with the arugula. So feel free to add those if you want. I would. And if you can't find Fourme d'Ambert, use blue cheese from the Auvergne, Roquefort, or Stilton. Or choose a great American blue, such as Humboldt Fog or Maytag.

Arugula Salad with Toasted Pecans, Blue Cheese, and Sherry Vinaigrette

1/4 cup	pecans
2 large bunches	arugula, plus other greens, if desired
1	red onion, thickly sliced
1	shallot, minced
3 tablespoons	Spanish sherry vinegar
1 tablespoon	red wine vinegar
	sea salt and freshly ground pepper
1/2 cup	extra virgin olive oil
4 ounces	blue cheese, such as Fourme d'Ambert, rind removed, crumbled

Preheat the oven to 300°F. Toast the pecans for 5 to 7 minutes, until ligtly browned and fragrant.

Wash and dry the arugula and other greens if using them, and place in a towel in the refrigerator until ready to make the salad.

Put a heavy skillet over medium heat until the pan is hot, about 2 minutes. Add the red onion. Cook for about 8 minutes, stirring constantly, until the slices are charred and softened. Let cool to room temperature.

To make the vinaigrette, put the shallot in a small mixing bowl. Add the sherry vinegar, red wine vinegar, and a pinch each of salt and pepper; let macerate for 15 minutes. Slowly whisk in the olive oil and taste to see if more salt and pepper are necessary.

Meanwhile, put the toasted pecans in a small bowl. Add a splash of olive oil and season lightly with salt and pepper.

To assemble the salad, put the arugula, red onion, toasted pecans, and blue cheese in a large bowl. Toss together just until mixed. Add the vinaigrette and toss again.

Divide the salad among 4 plates and offer with a glass of white wine.

Radicchio Salad with Melted Cheese Toasts

2 heads	radicchio, preferably variegato di Castelfranco, washed, drained upside down
2	clementines
2	Meyer lemons
2	cipolline or other sweet onions, halved and cut crosswise into 1/8-inch-thick slices
2 tablespoons	extra virgin olive oil
2 tablespoons	hazelnut or walnut oil
	fleur de sel and freshly ground pepper
1/2 pound	melting cheese, such as Italian fontina
8 to 12 slices	bread, 1/4 inch thick, diagonally cut from a baguette
1 tablespoon	fresh thyme flowers or leaves, chopped

Preheat the oven to 425°F.

Separate the leaves of the radicchio and put them in a salad bowl.

Peel the clementines and lemons down to the flesh. Cut off the tops and bottoms and, holding the fruit over a bowl, cut out the sections between the membranes, saving any juices. Put the segments in the bowl. Squeeze all the trimmings and collect that juice as well. Add the cipolline to the citrus segments.

Make a dressing of the collected citrus juices, olive oil, nut oil, salt, and pepper. Pour over the cipolline and the citrus sections and toss together.

Slice the cheese and arrange on the slices of bread. Bake in the oven until the cheese is melted and slightly golden, about 5 minutes.

Pour the dressed citrus and onion over the radicchio and toss well. Sprinkle with the thyme flowers, salt, and pepper. Serve the salad with the hot cheese toasts.

Never be afraid to use your fingers; they are the most accurate tool.
—MARK PEEL

As Mark Peel and I were walking around the Santa Monica Farmer's Market one January day, we saw the most beautiful radicchio I have ever seen. Don't get me wrong; I love the "*rosso precoce*" and its cousin, the shorter-leaved "*rosso tardivo*." But for the bunched radicchio, instead of the "di Chioggia" we are so used to, Mark chose the "variegato di Castelfranco," shaped like a Boston lettuce. With its light green, cream-colored leaves variegated with the red-purple of radicchio, it is spectacularly elegant.

Mark Peel's Radicchio Salad with Melted Cheese Toasts.

Shrimp Salad
on Cornbread Crostini

1	onion, peeled, coarsely chopped
1	celery rib, coarsely chopped
1 clove	garlic, crushed
1 small bundle	fresh thyme, leek leaves, and parsley
	salt
1 pound	fresh shrimp (26 to 30 count), preferably white Carolina
2 tablespoons	diced red bell pepper
1	scallion (white and tender green), finely chopped
1/2 tablespoon	chopped fresh parsley leaves
1 teaspoon	chopped fresh chives
1 teaspoon	chopped fresh tarragon leaves
2 tablespoons	mayonnaise
dash	Tabasco
1 recipe	Southern-Style Skillet Cornbread (page 66), cut into pieces 3 by 2 inches
4 sprigs	fresh chervil

Bring 2 quarts of water to a boil in a medium saucepan. Add the onion, celery, garlic, herb bundle, and 1 tablespoon salt. Reduce the heat and simmer for 15 minutes.

Add the shrimp and return to a boil. Immediately remove the saucepan from the heat and let the shrimp steep for 3 minutes. Drain and discard the herbs and vegetables. Peel and split the shrimp in half lengthwise; remove any veins.

Put the bell pepper, scallion, parsley, chives, tarragon, mayonnaise, and Tabasco in a medium bowl and mix together. Add the shrimp, toss, and taste to adjust the salt and Tabasco, if necessary.

Toast the cornbread for 3 minutes on each side and divide among 6 plates. Spoon the shrimp salad over the cornbread crostini. Garnish with the chervil sprigs or with more chives and parsley.

Heirloom Radish Salad with Basil and Meyer Lemon

JEREMIAH TOWER

SERVES 4

2	large watermelon radishes, peeled
2	Meyer lemons, juiced, zest removed and finely chopped
1/2 cup	organic, cold-pressed canola oil or yellow extra virgin olive oil
	sea salt
1 cup	fresh white goat cheese
1/2 cup	green pumpkin seeds, lightly toasted, finely chopped
	freshly ground white pepper
1/2 cup	micro basil or shredded basil leaves, preferably purple

Cut the radishes on a vegetable slicer into rounds 1/8 inch thick and put them in a bowl. Add the Meyer lemon juice, lemon zest, oil, and 2 pinches of sea salt. Toss and let stand for 5 minutes. Toss again and let stand for another 5 minutes.

Meanwhile, form the goat cheese into 4 round patties, about 1 1/2 inches thick. Roll in the chopped pumpkin seeds. Season with white pepper.

Lay the radish rounds on each of 4 large chilled white plates so that they form one layer. Place the goat cheese rounds in the center of the radish slices. Dress the basil with the remaining lemon dressing in the bowl and scatter it around and over the radish. Pour any remaining dressing from the bowl onto the cheese. Season with pepper and a little more sea salt and serve.

For this dish, use any of the large, new heirloom radishes, such as watermelon or Beauty Heart, with their beautiful, "tie-die" cross sections.

As for the organic, cold-pressed canola oil from Canada, run—don't walk—to find that, though you can substitute yellow extra virgin olive oil.

If you can't find Meyer lemons, use regular ones that are ripe and full of juice mixed with some freshly squeezed grapefruit juice; the proportions should be 2/3 lemon to 1/3 grapefruit juice.

Jeremiah, Patrick O'Connell, and guests at the Inn at Little Washington.

Patrick O'Connell The Inn at Little Washington, Virginia

IF YOU BELIEVE THAT GOD IS IN THE DETAILS, then Patrick O'Connell and Reinhardt Lynch's digs in Virginia, the Inn at Little Washington, are for you. The moment you arrive, the attention to detail is everywhere. It's not just the Dalmatian dogs dressed in black tie or the Dalmatian-dog-patterned chef pants on one of the best kitchen crews I have ever seen, nor is it the millions of dollars' worth of curtains. It is about, as D. H. Lawrence so often wrote, a sense of perfect place, and the obvious fact that Patrick and Reinhardt have made their place in this little town in the middle of everywhere. At the Inn at Little Washington, one can sink into the pleasures of perfectly managed luxury and feel suddenly normal or, at least, totally content with the world.

The day I was there the weather was bleak and cold, but when I sank into the richly upholstered armchair at breakfast, in a nook of the luxurious dining room that overlooked the garden court, I knew even before tasting any food that I was in a world I never wanted to leave. Then when I tasted pastries as perfect as I have ever eaten, I knew that if I didn't stand up, they wouldn't be able to get me out of the chair. The waiters are always there when you need them, and a few times when you do not, offering yet another tray of hot hors d'oeuvres or, later, an endless parade of buttery cookies, petits fours, and hand-crafted chocolates.

Patrick can take a humble ingredient like rutabaga (chosen for family memories, the region, and the winter season) and combine it with maple syrup to make a brilliant match between rusticity and refinement. Later, in the sunny, if brisk, January garden with a glass of champagne in one hand and a Dalmatian dog by the other, I asked Patrick what the secret was in having the world beat a path to his doors every day of the year.

"Jeremiah, it's all in the details."

"Yes," I agreed, loosening my belt a notch, "and there isn't one we have seen here that wasn't perfect. I'll be back, but don't ever expect me to leave."

The dog, now with both of my hands scratching its ears, agreed.

Apple and Rutabaga Soup

PATRICK O'CONNELL

MAKES 2 QUARTS;
6 TO 8 SERVINGS

1/4 pound	unsalted butter
1	large onion, peeled, coarsely chopped
2	Granny Smith apples, peeled, cored, coarsely chopped
1	rutabaga, peeled, coarsely chopped
1	small buttercup squash, peeled, seeded, coarsely chopped
4	large carrots, peeled, coarsely chopped
1	large sweet potato, peeled, coarsely chopped
	salt
4 cups	Rich Brown Chicken Stock (page 193)
2 cups	heavy cream
1/4 cup	maple syrup
	cayenne

Here's a wonderful simple soup with all the flavors of fall. It can be made vegetarian by substituting vegetable stock for the chicken stock.

Melt the butter in a large saucepan over medium-high heat. As soon as it melts, add the onion, apples, rutabaga, squash, carrots, sweet potato, and 1/2 teaspoon salt. Reduce the heat to medium-low and cook for 10 minutes, stirring occasionally, until the onions are translucent but not brown.

Add the chicken stock and bring to a boil. Simmer for 20 to 25 minutes, or until all the vegetables are tender when pierced with a fork. Remove from the heat.

When the vegetables are cool enough to handle, puree them through the fine blade of a food mill, in a food processor, or briefly in a blender. Strain the puree back into the cooking pot and discard what's left in the sieve.

Add the cream and maple syrup to the soup. Season with a pinch of cayenne and more salt if necessary, remembering that when you reheat the soup, the seasoning will be more powerful. Return the pot to the stove and reheat, without letting it boil. Serve hot.

PHILIPPE BOULOT

SERVES 4

Serving rich soup in a demi-tasse or coffee cup is not new, but it's still a lot of fun and clearly not a fad—it's here to stay. Turning the soup into a "cappuccino" and serving what looks like a brew that should be served at ten o'clock in the morning adds to the surprise and certainly to the enjoyment. Here, Philippe serves the soup in open soup plates, since it is easier to eat the mushrooms and duck liver.

Tip: For convenience, the stock can be made a day or two ahead.

Wild Mushroom and Foie Gras Cappuccino

1/2 pound	fresh foie gras, cut on the bias into 8 medallions 3/4 inch thick
2 tablespoons	sliced shallots
2 teaspoons	chopped mixed fresh herbs: thyme, parsley, tarragon
1/4 pound	wild mushrooms (chanterelles, black trumpets, morels), thinly sliced
	sea salt and freshly ground pepper
1 cup	ruby port
2 cups	Quick Meat Stock (recipe follows)
1	large plum tomato, peeled, seeded, and chopped
1 cup	heavy cream, whipped

Sear the duck liver medallions in a hot sauté pan for 10 seconds on each side. Transfer them to a warm plate and set aside.

Cook the shallots and herbs in the rendered liver fat over low heat for 3 minutes. Add the mushrooms and cook over medium heat, stirring, for another 5 minutes, or until softened. Season with salt and pepper.

Meanwhile, boil the port until reduced by half. Bring the meat stock to a simmer. Add the reduced port and season with salt and pepper to taste.

Divide the mushrooms among 4 hot soup plates. Place the foie gras on top and sprinkle the tomato around the edge.

Whisk the whipped cream vigorously into the simmering stock for a few seconds to create a foam. Set the plates in front of your guests and immediately ladle the "port cappuccino soup" over the mushrooms and foie gras. Serve at once.

Quick Meat Stock

1	large onion, chopped
2 tablespoons	vegetable oil
1 pound	ground beef
	mushroom trimmings (whatever you have)
2 cups	Rich Brown Chicken Stock (page 193)

MAKES ABOUT 1 CUP

Cook the onion in the vegetable oil in a medium saucepan over low heat, covered, stirring occasionally, until soft, about 5 minutes. Then raise the heat to medium and cook, stirring often to prevent burning, until the onion is "caramelized" and a deep golden brown, about 15 minutes. Remove and set aside.

Put the beef in the same pan and sear over high heat until crusty and browned. Then add the mushroom trimmings and browned onions and cook together 5 minutes longer. Pour the chicken stock over the beef mixture, bring to a boil, and immediately lower to a bare simmer. Skim off any scum or fat that rises to the surface and cook for 1 1/2 hours.

Strain through a fine-mesh sieve and discard the cooked beef and onion. Let the beef stock cool, then refrigerate or freeze.

Philippe Boulot's Wild Mushroom and Foie Gras Cappucino.

Philippe Boulot The Heathman Restaurant, Portland, Oregon

FROM THE MOMENT I ARRIVED IN PORTLAND TO COOK WITH PHILIPPE BOULOT at The Heathman Restaurant, the staff started to apologize for the weather. But later, on my way through the Willamette Valley to cook with Philippe at the Willakenzie Winery, I told him I thought that pinot noir (the local specialty) always tastes better in slightly gray, chilled, and rainy weather, and that the dishes Philippe had chosen to prepare—creamed sole with fresh Oregon black truffles and venison with wild mushrooms—were perfect for the weather, the setting, and the wine.

As a chef, Philippe was classically trained in France, and he loves the old dishes of both *la grande cuisine* (formal French cuisine, usually found in restaurants) and the cuisine of *grandmere* (or home cooking). I think he was a bit nervous about suggesting that we cook a cream and butter sauce for the fish. After all, I am from California, the land of "light" food.

What he did not know was that I have an infinitely large soft spot in my heart for the same food that he loves. And when Philippe told the story of his Norman grandmother making cream in big barrels, my mouth started to water, and the sole *normande* put a smile on my face. America (or New England, at least) has always had a tradition of fish in cream sauces, which no doubt originated with the French versions of *à la dieppoise* (mussles and cream) and *normande* (the aforementioned *dieppoise* with black truffles added). The flavor magic of white wine, shallots, essence of mussels, fresh thyme, and cream won over everyone, even those who would swear they could never enjoy rich cream sauces.

But the Tarte Tatin he made for dessert had no such preconceptions to overcome. This sweet is surely a contender for the top ten most delicious desserts in the world, and usually no one can resist this upside-down tart of apples cooked in their own juices with sugar and butter. The guests at the lunch were no exception to the rule. It was blustery, blowing, and gun-metal gray outside; but as the aromas of buttery pastry and hot caramelized apples wafted around the room, even the most satiated of appetites sprang back into action. Traditional flavors had struck again.

Philippe summed it up when he said that he feels the secret of his success at The Heathman is in his using French technique combined with local, fresh ingredients from Oregon. It's how the revolution in the way America dines started thirty years ago, and it is obviously alive and well in Philippe's northwestern kitchen. Traditional comfort is what Philippe's Heathman dining room is all about as well. Its décor is tempered by the stunning paintings on the walls, creating a room to match Philippe: unpretentious and refined but lighthearted. Philippe learned "exactitude and discipline" from Paris's Joël Robuchon, and "wild creativity" from another Paris chef, Alain Senderens. Put those influences together in Philippe, and you have a chef who says that it is all about "having fun."

I certainly did with him.

ALAIN DUCASSE

SERVES 4

In Alain Ducasse's monumental new cookbook *Grand livre de cusine*, this soup appears as *Cresson de fontaine*, but he also calls it a velouté. He's not referring to velouté as the soup classically thickened with flour and butter and cooked for hours to obtain a velvet texture, but to the texture itself—slightly thick and certainly velvety.

As for the osetra caviar, it comes from a sturgeon not as large as the beluga; its prices are not as enormous, either. Osetra is famous for its value and for its nutty taste—a perfect match for the brown butter used in the watercress puree.

Watercress Soup with Sea Scallops and Osetra Caviar

4 cups	unsalted chicken stock
1/2 pound	spinach leaves, stemmed, washed, drained
2 bunches	watercress, tough stems removed, washed, drained
8	sea scallops, tough bit on side removed, rinsed, patted dry
1	lemon, juiced
1/4 cup	extra virgin olive oil
5 ounces	osetra caviar
3/4 cup	Brown Butter (page 202)
	sea salt and freshly ground pepper
1/2 cup	unsweetened whipped cream

Boil the chicken stock in a medium saucepan until reduced by half to 2 cups.

Meanwhile, in a large saucepan, boil the spinach and watercress in 5 quarts of heavily salted water until the leaves disintegrate between your fingers, about 5 minutes. Drain, cool rapidly in ice-cold water, and drain again. Press lightly to remove excess water. Puree the leaves in a blender and strain through a fine sieve.

Slice each scallop into 3 thin rounds. Mix the lemon juice and olive oil together and dip the scallop rounds in this mixture before putting them on a nonreactive metal or glass tray. Spoon 3/4 of the caviar onto 12 of the rounds, dividing it evenly; place the other scallop rounds on top. Distribute the remainder of the caviar equally on top of the 12 little scallop-caviar "sandwiches."

Return the reduced stock to a boil and whisk in the brown butter. Add the watercress puree, season with salt, and grind in quite a lot of pepper. Puree the mixture in a blender or food processor until well emulsified.

Place 3 scallop sandwiches in a triangle on each of 4 warm plates. Heat the watercress puree and pour it around the scallops. Spoon a dollop of whipped cream into the center around, but not on top of, the scallops and sprinkle the cream with very coarse freshly ground black pepper.

America's Best Chefs Cook *with* Jeremiah Tower

Wild Sand Plum Dessert Soup with Persimmon Cream

JEREMIAH TOWER

SERVES 4

1/2 cup	dried, organic, sulfur-free persimmons
2 cups	light simple syrup*
1/4 cup	fresh or dried heavily scented red or pink rose petals
2	ripe red Bartlett pears
1 cup	thick crème fraîche, sour cream, or mascarpone
	salt
2 cups	sweetened plum puree (see note at right)
1/4 cup	wild huckleberry puree, strained
8	sugared rose petals (optional)

In a small saucepan, combine the persimmons with 1 cup of the syrup. Simmer for 10 minutes. Remove from the heat and puree to the point that there are still a few small chunks of persimmon. Strain, reserving the puree and the chunks separately.

Warm the remaining 1 cup syrup in a small saucepan and add the rose petals. Remove from the heat and let stand for 15 minutes.

Cut the pears in half; remove the stem, core, and seeds. Pass the fruit through a mandoline or vegetable cutter to make 1/8-inch sticks. Put the pear sticks in the rose syrup.

Mix the chunked persimmon with the crème fraîche. Add just enough of the persimmon puree so that it flavors the cream without thinning it down too much. Mix in a pinch of salt.

Divide the plum puree among 4 large, chilled soup plates. Spoon the persimmon cream into the center. Drain the pears with the rose petals and spoon them over the cream. Drizzle a little of the remaining persimmon puree over the pears. Then drizzle on the huckleberry puree. Decorate the top of each with 2 of the sugared rose petals.

To make a light simple syrup, combine 1 cup sugar and 1 cup water in a small saucepan. Bring to a boil, stirring to dissolve the syrup. Remove from the heat and let cool. This can be made days ahead and stored in a covered jar in the refrigerator.

When cooking with Odessa Piper at her restaurant, L'Etoile, in Madison, Wisconsin, we talked about Euell Gibbons' *Stalking the Wild Asparagus,* and how much it had been an inspiration in the seventies when we started cooking. So in the middle of winter, I stalked her kitchen and came up with some amazing ingredients she had put away to save the flavors of summer for the winter menus. The wild sand plum puree she had frozen was one of the best fruit flavors I had ever tasted. Right, I thought, a soup!

If you don't have sand plums, use the ripest, most flavorful, plums you can find at a farmer's market, cook them with sugar for 10 minutes, puree, and use fresh or freeze. The amount of sugar added should leave the puree still with a good bite of acidity.

PATRICK O'CONNELL

SERVES 6

It is important that Virginia ham be sliced as thinly as one would prosciutto, so that the textures of the ham and the pear are similar to each other. If you don't have a mechanical slicer, it is best to have it sliced thinly where you buy it.

Pear, Virginia Ham, Parmigiano-Reggiano, and Arugula Salad

3	ripe Anjou pears
8-ounce chunk	Parmigiano-Reggiano cheese
6 ounces	Virginia country ham or prosciutto, sliced paper thin
1 large bunch	young arugula, stemmed, washed, spin-dried
1/4 cup	pine nuts, toasted
1 cup	yellow extra virgin olive oil
	freshly cracked pepper

Peel the pears. Slice them very thinly by shaving them on 4 sides on a mandoline or Japanese vegetable cutter. Then slice the cheese the same way or with a cheese slicer.

Delicately layer the pear, ham, cheese, arugula, and pine nuts in a mound in the center of each of 6 room-temperature plates. Drizzle with the olive oil, sprinkle with pepper, and serve.

Pasta, Breads, and Grains

Pasta "Moulinier Style"

ALAIN DUCASSE

SERVES 4

The interesting thing about this dish is that it cooks dried pasta just like risotto. Because of the initial sautéing in olive oil, butter, and aromatics and the gradual additions of liquid, the resulting texture is al dente.

3 tablespoons	olive oil
6 tablespoons	unsalted butter
1 bunch	scallions, cut into 2-inch pieces
1/4 pound	red onion, thinly sliced
1/4 pound	yellow, waxy potatoes, peeled, cut in 1/4-inch-thick slices
14 ounces	tubular artisanal durum wheat pasta, such as macaroni or penne
	salt and freshly ground pepper
1 clove	garlic, peeled
1 large sprig	fresh basil, stemmed, stems and leaves saved
2	large ripe, red tomatoes, cored, quartered
4 cups	Rich Brown Chicken Stock (page 193)
1/4 cup	freshly grated Parmigiano-Reggiano

Heat half the olive oil in a large nonreactive skillet. Add the butter and as soon as it melts, add the scallions and red onion. Cover and sweat over low heat just until soft, about 4 minutes.

Add the potatoes, stir, and cook uncovered over medium heat for another 3 minutes, stirring the vegetables several times with a spatula.

Add the pasta, a little salt and pepper, the garlic, and the basil stems. Cook, stirring as if cooking a risotto, for 5 minutes. Then add the tomatoes and cook for another 3 minutes.

Add 1 cup of the chicken stock. Cook at a low simmer, adding more of the chicken stock about 1/2 cup at a time and stirring gently, until the pasta is completely cooked, another 10 to 15 minutes. Remove and discard the garlic clove and basil stems.

Cut the basil leaves into strips about 1/4 inch wide.

Sprinkle the cheese over the pasta and mix it in gently. Add half the remaining olive oil and the cut basil leaves and mix in delicately. Check for seasoning. Divide among 4 heated open soup plates. Drizzle the remaining olive oil on top, add a grinding of pepper, and serve immediately.

Italian Potato Dumplings

PHILIPPE BOULOT

2 pounds	baking potatoes, peeled, quartered
2	whole eggs
2	egg yolks
1 teaspoon	salt
	freshly ground white pepper
1 1/2 cups	all-purpose flour
1/4 cup	olive oil

SERVES 4 TO 6

This is a recipe that allows you to prepare the dumplings in advance. Reheat them briefly in simmering water and serve with your favorite sauce—tomato, cream, meat, or game.

Preheat the oven to 250°F. Boil the potatoes in salted water until thoroughly cooked but not falling apart, 10 to 15 minutes. Drain them and place on a sheet pan to dry.

Put the pan of potatoes in the oven and dry further for 20 minutes, being careful not to let them brown or form a skin. Pass the potatoes through a ricer or the coarse holes of a food mill into the bowl of an electric mixer; let cool.

Add the whole eggs, egg yolks, salt, and a pinch of white pepper to the potatoes and mix with the dough hook attachment, or beat with a wooden spoon. Gradually add 1/2 cup of the flour and mix on low speed until all the flour is incorporated. Speed up the mixer slightly and gradually add another 1/2 cup flour or enough to form a soft, sticky dough.

Turn the dough out onto a work surface covered with the remaining flour. Take pieces of the dough and roll out into long ropes about 1/2 inch in diameter, using flour to facilitate the rolling. Cut on the diagonal using the dull edge of a spatula or knife. Toss the dumplings in the flour to keep them separate.

Bring a large wide saucepan or flameproof casserole of salted water to a low simmer. Add the dumplings in batches and cook until they float to the top. Taste one: If it is still floury, cook for another 15 seconds. Remove with a large skimmer or slotted spoon and plunge into ice water to cool for 10 seconds. Drain on towels, then toss in a bowl very gently with the olive oil to keep them from sticking together. Repeat with the remaining dumplings. They are now ready to be reheated with your favorite sauce or gratinéed with butter and cheese.

ROBERT MCGRATH

SERVES 4

This dish is served with Roaring Fork's Grilled Duck Breasts with Green Chile Macaroni on page 101, but since Robert cooks the macaroni in individual ramekins, it could easily be served by itself as a lunch course with a salad.

Robert advises, when using poblano (or any chile), tasting a piece of each one of them, since they vary greatly in heat, even from the same field.

You will need 4 individual ramekins 3 inches deep and 2 to 3 inches in diameter, or use one larger casserole.

MICHAEL ROMANO

SERVES 4

Bottarga is fish roe, usually from tuna, that is pressed and salted. It is commonly found in Italian markets and specialty food stores. In Italy, it has been called "Sicilian caviar," since Sicily is traditionally where the tuna is caught. The roe can be eaten

Green Chile Macaroni

1/4 cup	olive oil
1/2 cup	seeded, finely chopped fresh poblano pepper
1 tablespoon	finely chopped garlic
1 cup	heavy cream
1/2 cup	grated pepperjack cheese
	salt and freshly ground pepper
3 cups	cooked macaroni, tossed in olive oil when drained
1/2 cup	grated dry Jack cheese

Preheat the oven to 375°F.

Heat the olive oil in a large sauté pan over medium heat. Add the poblano, reduce the heat to low, and cook for 2 minutes. Add the garlic, stir, and cook until the chile is soft. Then add 3/4 cup of the cream. Cook for another 3 minutes. Mix in the pepperjack cheese. As soon as the cheese melts, stir in the cooked macaroni. Season with salt and pepper to taste.

Spoon the macaroni into 4 individual ramekins. Cover the tops with the dry Jack cheese. Bake in the oven for 15 minutes, or until the dish is heated through and bubbling and the cheese is golden and crusty on top.

Spaghetti with Oven-Dried Tomatoes and Bottarga

2/3 cup	fresh white bread crumbs
5 tablespoons	chopped fresh Italian parsley leaves
3/4 cup	extra virgin olive oil
	sea salt and freshly ground pepper
12 ounces	best-quality spaghetti, preferably imported
1/2 cup	Oven-Cooked Tomatoes (page 146)
1 tablespoon	fresh oregano leaves, chopped
1/2 cup	bottarga, skin removed, finely chopped
2 tablespoons	finely chopped garlic

Preheat the oven to 400°F. Put on 6 quarts of salted water to boil in a large pot.

Mix the bread crumbs with 3 tablespoons of the parsley, 1/4 cup of the olive oil, and a pinch each salt and pepper. Spread out on a baking tray and toast in the oven for 10 minutes, or until just golden and crisp. Remove from the oven and keep warm.

Cook the spaghetti in the boiling water until al dente, 10 to 15 minutes. (Imported artisinal pasta will be on the long side, while more commercial brands will not take more than 10 or 12 minutes.)

Meanwhile, warm 1/4 cup olive oil in a large sauté pan over medium heat. Add the tomatoes and oregano. Cook for 1 minute while stirring. Add the *bottarga*, garlic, and remaining 2 tablespoons parsley. Cook for another minute and add 1/4 cup of the pasta boiling water so that the ingredients do not "fry" in the olive oil but begin to make a sauce.

When the spaghetti is done, drain it and add to the sauce. Add the remaining 1/4 cup olive oil and cook, tossing, for 1 minute. Serve in a heated bowl with the warm seasoned bread crumbs sprinkled over the top.

as is—on toasts or as shaved slices mixed with very thinly sliced celery, olive oil, and pepper—or shaved over other foods. It is usually accompanied in some way by garlic and parsley, and sometimes peperoncino, dried hot red pepper.

Use the best-quality *bottarga* and olive oil, since they are the main flavorings. The dish is finished with parslied bread crumbs for added texture and flavor.

Michael Romano's Spaghetti with Oven-Dried Tomatoes and Bottarga.

Lemon-Chive Seafood Risotto

RICK TRAMONTO

SERVES 6 TO 8

At TRU, Rick serves this risotto with a "saffron emulsion" over and around the rice and shellfish. But the risotto is quite delicious without it.

1 bunch	fresh chives
1	lemon, zested
1/2 pound	unsalted butter (2 sticks), at room temperature
1 cup	Arborio rice
1 1/2 cups	dry white wine
4 to 6 cups	Vegetable Stock (page 193)
1/4 cup	olive oil
1/4 pound	fresh squid, cleaned, cut crosswise in 1/4-inch strips
8	small sea scallops (or 4 large, sliced in half horizontally)
16	spot prawns, shelled
16	mussels, washed, bearded
1 cup	freshly grated Parmigiano-Reggiano
3/4 cup	Whipped Cream (page 208)
	salt and freshly ground pepper

Make a chive butter: Dip the chives in boiling water for 20 seconds, drain, and put into a food processor. Puree for 1 minute. Add the lemon zest and all but 2 tablespoons of the butter. Process for several minutes, until very smooth and green. Cover and refrigerate.

Rick Tramonto's Lemon-Chive Seafood Risotto.

America's Best Chefs Cook *with* Jeremiah Tower

Put the rice and the remaining 2 tablespoons butter in a large, heavy saucepan over medium heat. Cook, stirring, until all the butter has melted and the grains of rice are translucent, about 6 minutes.

Pour in 1 cup of the wine and cook, still stirring, until the wine has evaporated. Add 1 cup of the stock and continue to cook and stir, adding another 1 cup stock as the liquid evaporates, until the rice is al dente and the sauce is thick but still slightly soupy, 15 to 20 minutes.

When the rice is almost done, in between stirrings, heat the olive oil in a large frying pan over medium-high heat. Add the squid, scallops, prawns, and mussels, and cook for 2 minutes, stirring occasionally. Add the remaining 1/2 cup white wine and cook for another minute.

When the rice is still just a little bit al dente, mix in the cheese. Fold in the chive butter and whipped cream, and taste for seasoning. Serve in warmed soup plates, with the seafood and its juices on top of the rice.

Spoonbread

8 tablespoons	butter (1 stick), cut into tablespoons
4 cups	water
2 cups	stone-ground yellow cornmeal
1 cup	heavy cream
1 cup	buttermilk
7	eggs
1/4 cup	freshly grated Parmigiano-Reggiano
1 teaspoon	salt
1/4 teaspoon	freshly ground white pepper

Preheat the oven to 400°F.

Bring the butter and water to a boil in a 3-quart saucepan. When the butter is completely melted, slowly and gradually swirl in the cornmeal. Cook over medium heat, stirring or whisking all the time, for 3 to 5 minutes, or until thick and smooth. Stir in the cream and buttermilk. Remove from the heat and let cool.

Whisk in the eggs and then the cheese, salt, and white pepper.

Butter a 3-quart casserole and pour in the spoonbread. Bake until just set, 20 to 25 minutes.

FRANK STITT

SERVES 4 TO 6

Frank serves this soft cornbread with Louisiana Rabbit with Wild Mushrooms, which you'll find on page 106. It would also go well with roast chicken, fried fish, or even Thanksgiving dinner.

JEREMIAH TALKS ABOUT
Charlie Trotter   Charlie Trotter's, Chicago

GREAT RESTAURANT-OWNING CHEFS ARE SATISFIED WITH NOTHING LESS than creating their own universe within their walls, and Charlie Trotter is no exception to the rule. Part of the pleasure of experiencing their worlds is the surprise one feels on first seeing the location.

(Above and at right) Jeremiah cooking with Charlie Trotter at Trotter's restaurant in Chicago.

The exterior of Charlie Trotter's townhouse restaurant in Chicago has nothing of the glamour of Miracle Mile (a mile or so away), just some steps up to residential-looking front doors, which give no clue to the world of hand-crafted and artistic activity on the other side.

When I arrived there, Charlie and his staff were putting on a full-service dinner for twenty high-school students in the demonstration kitchen/dining room, as they do a few times a week. The other dining rooms were packed, and what really impressed me was that the students were getting exactly the same amount of attention given to the paying guests. The high-school group was also being served the same food—all explained in passionate detail by Charlie.

Sinking back into the comforts of the oasis called Charlie Trotter's that night, I tucked into a plate of hot foie gras, followed by some perfect risotto, then beef filet with arugula-flavored polenta cakes and yellowfoot mushroom sauce. Finally came a procession of desserts, which included molasses spice cake with caramelized quince, burnt orange caramel, and maple mascarpone cream. Every dish was carefully calculated to express the character of each perfect ingredient as well as the harmony of them all brought together on a plate.

Suffice it to say, the point of the universe created by a great restaurateur is to make one feel, out of the time beyond its walls, that all is right with the world. Charlie does that.

Crisp Arugula-Polenta Cakes

1 tablespoon	salt
2 tablespoons	extra virgin olive oil
2 cups	coarse-grained polenta or instant polenta
8 tablespoons	butter (1 stick)
1 cup	arugula leaves, coarsely chopped
	freshly ground white pepper

Boil 6 cups of water with the salt and the olive oil. Transfer 2 cups to a heatproof glass measuring cup. With the remaining water still boiling, gradually sprinkle in the cornmeal, stirring constantly. Keep adding and stirring, paying particular attention to the corners of the pan so no polenta sticks there and burns. When all the polenta has been added, reduce the heat to a simmer and continue to cook, stirring every 5 minutes, until the polenta is soft, creamy, and tender, about another 30 to 40 minutes, or 10 for the instant. If the polenta becomes too thick (it should be like porridge), add additional hot water.

While the polenta is cooking, use 1 tablespoon of the butter to grease a large baking sheet: chill in the refrigerator.

When the polenta is cooked, stir in the chopped arugula and 6 tablespoons of the butter. Season with salt and white pepper. Pour the polenta onto the chilled baking sheet and smooth it evenly. Smear the remaining 1 tablespoon butter over the surface. Let cool, then cover the sheet with plastic film and refrigerate until firm. Cut into squares or rounds until needed for reheating in olive oil or butter.

Crisp Polenta

1 1/2 cups	water
1/2 cup	polenta
	salt and freshly ground pepper
1/4 cup	Garlic Puree (page 206)
4 tablespoons	unsalted butter

Bring the water to a boil in a medium saucepan. Slowly add the polenta, stirring all the time. Simmer over low heat, while still stirring, for

Continued

CHARLIE TROTTER

SERVES 4 TO 6

Charlie serves these crisp polenta cakes with the Beef Tenderloin with Yellowfoot Mushrooms on page 112, but they will go with almost any ragout.

The polenta should be made a day ahead to let it firm up, then cut out and sautéed or baked again when needed. Once it has set and you want soft creamy polenta again, reheat it with enough hot water to thin to the desired consistency; it will stay soft in a double boiler for hours, never to harden again.

Of course, for extra flavor, you could add 1/2 cup freshly grated Parmigiano-Reggiano to the polenta at the end with the butter. If you do so, reduce the amount of butter to 4 tablespoons.

CHARLIE TROTTER

SERVES 4

Charlie serves polenta crisped in butter with a rack of lamb (page 127), but it goes well with any grilled or braised meat, like Philippe Boulot's Seven-Hour Braised Leg of Lamb on page 122.

30 minutes, or until the polenta is soft and begins to pull away from the sides of the pan. Season with salt and pepper to taste.

Mix the garlic puree and 2 tablespoons of the butter into the cooked polenta and season again with salt and pepper.

Spread the polenta into a plastic wrap-lined 8-inch-square baking pan. Spread 1 tablespoon of the butter on top; cover and refrigerate for 2 hours.

When the polenta is cooled and firm, cut it into four 3-inch circles. Cook the polenta rounds in the remaining 1 tablespoon butter in a large skillet over medium-high heat for 3 minutes on each side, or until golden brown and crisp.

Southern-Style Skillet Cornbread

JEREMIAH TOWER

SERVES 6

$1/4$ cup	rendered bacon fat
$1^1/2$ cups	white or yellow stone-ground cornmeal
$3/4$ cup	all-purpose flour
1 tablespoon	sugar
2 teaspoons	baking powder
$1/2$ teaspoon	baking soda
$3/4$ teaspoon	salt
1	large egg
$1/4$ cup	melted butter
1 cup	buttermilk

To go all the way Southern style, one can make "cracklin' bread," a cornbread into which the "cracklins" or crunchy bits of pork left over in the rendering pots are mixed into the batter. Here I use rendered bacon fat.

You can use white or yellow cornmeal, but by all means choose the best quality stone-ground meal available.

Preheat the oven to 425°F. Put the bacon fat in a seasoned cast-iron skillet and place the pan in the oven to heat while you make the batter.

Put the cornmeal, flour, sugar, baking powder, baking soda, and salt in a mixing bowl. Mix the egg, butter, and buttermilk in a separate bowl; beat until blended, then slowly stir into the cornmeal mix. Pour the batter into the hot skillet and return the skillet to the oven.

Bake for 25 minutes, or until the cornbread is golden on top and a thin skewer inserted into the center comes out clean.

Fish and Shellfish

FRANK STITT

SERVES 6

Baked Oysters with
Mustard Greens and Bacon

If you do not have young
mustard greens, use a mixture of half watercress and
half spinach, boiled together
for 1 minute, drained,
squeezed dry, and finely
chopped.

¹/₄ pound	apple- or hickory-smoked bacon, finely diced
1	small onion, finely diced
2	shallots, finely diced
2 cloves	garlic, finely diced
1	hot chile pepper, seeded, finely chopped
4 cups	young mustard greens, washed, drained, finely chopped
1	lemon, zested and juiced
	zest and juice of 1 lemon
¹/₄ pound	unsalted butter (1 stick)
	salt and freshly ground pepper
24	oysters on the half-shell (Bluepoint, Pemaquid, or Apalachicola)
1 cup	coarse white bread crumbs, from 1- or 2-day-old French bread, crusts removed

Preheat the oven to 500°F.

Cook the bacon in a large dry sauté pan over medium heat until the
fat is rendered and the bacon is almost crisp, about 5 minutes. Remove
the bacon with a slotted spoon and drain on paper towels.

Add the onion to the bacon fat in the pan and cook over medium-low
heat until very soft but not brown, 7 to 10 minutes. Add the shallots,
garlic, and chile and cook for another 2 minutes. Add the mustard
greens, lemon zest and juice, cooked bacon, and butter. Toss together
for about 1 minute to combine. Season the greens with salt and pepper.

Place a little mound of the dressed greens on each oyster. Sprinkle the
bread crumbs on top. Put the oysters on a baking sheet and bake in
the oven until the crumbs are golden and the oysters are heated through,
about 5 minutes.

Baked Oysters with Pancetta

JEREMIAH TOWER

SERVES 4

2	large red onions, thinly sliced
	salt
12	large Bluepoint or Apalachicola oysters
	rock salt
1 tablespoon	freshly grated lemon zest
12 thin slices	pancetta
2 tablespoons	coarsely chopped Italian parsley leaves
1 teaspoon	finely minced fresh red chilies (seeds and stems removed)

Preheat the oven to 425°F.

Cook the red onions in a large frying pan with $1/4$ cup water and a pinch of salt over low heat, covered, until completely soft, 10 to 15 minutes. Then uncover, raise the heat to medium, and cook, stirring all the time, until the onions are nut brown and caramelized.

Shuck the oysters, leaving them on the half-shell and reserving any oyster liquor. Fill 4 gratin dishes half full with rock salt and put them in the oven to heat.

Spoon the browned onions over the oysters, sprinkle with the lemon zest and any reserved oyster liquor, and then place a coiled slice of pancetta on top of each. Remove the gratin dishes from the oven, quickly nestle 3 oysters into the salt in each dish, and return them to the oven. Bake for 10 minutes.

Transfer gratin dishes to serving plates—a napkin folded in the center will cushion them and looks nice, too. Sprinkle the oysters first with chopped parsley, then with the chilies, and serve at once.

I wanted to cook something in Frank's Bistro, so I went "shopping" down the kitchen line to see what had already been prepped and was waiting to be made into the various dishes on the menu. I found oysters, of course, sliced pancetta (unsmoked Italian bacon), some caramelized onions, chopped red chilies, and chopped parsley. So I made up this dish. I use large oysters for cooking, since they shrink down to a manageable size, while little ones would disappear.

You will need 4 ovenproof gratin dishes just large enough to hold 3 oysters each and some rock salt.

KEN ORINGER

SERVES 4 TO 6

Ken serves this dish with tempura-fried fresh squash or zucchini blossoms either on top of the eels as a final garnish or as a side dish. In either case, sprinkle the blossoms with fleur de sel the moment they are cooked and serve them immediately.

Have all the ingredients ready to cook, because the dish takes just a few minutes to finish. And since the olive oil is basically the sauce, use the best quality you can find.

Glass Eel "Linguine" with Surf Clams

1	small Hokigai or Japanese red surf clam
1	small white surf clam
1/2 cup	extra virgin olive oil
4 cloves	garlic, sliced very thinly
2 cups	glass (baby) eels
2 ounces	Spanish ham, sliced very thinly
1 tablespoon	crushed hot red pepper
2 tablespoons	finely chopped fresh chives
	fleur de sel sea salt

Slice the outer solid parts of the clams (not the soft belly) into strips 2 inches long and 1/16 inch wide.

Put half the olive oil in a large nonstick skillet and heat until it sizzles when a drop of water is sprinkled into it. Then add the garlic slices, reduce the heat, and gently cook the garlic until it takes on a light brown color, 3 to 5 minutes.

The moment the garlic is colored, add the glass eels, raise the heat to medium-high, and cook, tossing all the time, until they are opaque, 2 to 3 minutes. Immediately transfer the eels to a heated mixing bowl and add the clams, ham, hot pepper, chives, and the remainder of the olive oil. Toss gently. Serve immediately in heated soup plates, with some fleur de sel sprinkled on top.

JEREMIAH TALKS ABOUT
Ken Oringer Clio, Boston

WHEN KEN ORINGER WALKS TOWARD YOU THROUGH THE DINING ROOM OF CLIO, his restaurant in Boston, he does not fill the room as most top chef-owners do. Perhaps it is the handsome, very youthful face, perhaps the modesty of his body language. But when he stands in front of you, the smile takes over, and you feel genuine enthusiasm, passion, and firmly gentle determination. And when I tasted my first bite of food—black bass and lemon tempura with Korean smoked salt—I knew I was in the hands of a master.

(Above, at left, and below) Jeremiah and Ken Oringer barbecuing a suckling pig on the beach in Scituate, Massachusetts.

The dish was one of the best ever put in front of me because of the discipline it exhibited (with a form of cooking very hard to control) in successfully bringing together several—but not too many—flavors. Each one works to the whole experience, and I could not help but think of Ken as von Karajan and his kitchen as the Berlin Philharmonic. Here was a chef, I thought, who could put together a single opus, as it were, but with all the instruments individually heard.

Clio's champagne-colored dining room walks the same line. As Ken can take a classic dish and make it undeniably one of his own without losing any of the honesty of flavors that made the original favorite, so he has made Clio his contemporary own without losing any of what we all love about the comfort and reassurance of an old-world dining room.

Oringer is one of the few chefs who is comfortable walking that very fine line (some might say a tightrope) between a chef who does just enough to a perfect ingredient and one who, with a stroke of the hand, does far too much. His "linguine" with clams is proof: not pasta, but linguine-looking juvenile eels with garlic, surf clams, red chili flakes and the best olive oil I have tasted in years.

Nothing more—and nothing more was needed.

MICHAEL ROMANO

SERVES 4

This dish is a Mediterranean-style *confit* of fresh cod, with a simple fresh tomato sauce. Once you have tried the texture and flavor of the fish cooked at low temperature in olive oil, you will always want to use this method for cooking cod.

The olive oil can be strained, refrigerated, and used again for frying squid or other fish. And I would suggest putting the fish in the oil when the fish is cold from the refrigerator, just in case the oil is too hot, so that the fish will cool the oil. Or use a deep-frying thermometer to be perfectly sure. The oil should be 180° to 190°F.

Michael Romano's Fresh Cod Poached in Extra Virgin Olive Oil.

Fresh Cod Poached in Extra Virgin Olive Oil

4 cups plus 2 tablespoons	yellow extra virgin olive oil
4 pieces	fresh cod fillet, 4 to 6 ounces each, cut from the thick end
	sea salt and freshly ground pepper
6	scallions, chopped
2 cloves	garlic, finely chopped
1/4 cup	fresh basil leaves, shredded
1 cup	chopped, peeled, seeded ripe tomatoes
1 1/2 teaspoons	Chianti vinegar or red wine vinegar
	basil leaves or herb flowers, for garnish

Heat 4 cups of the olive oil in a 2- to 3-quart saucepan to 180°F on a deep-frying thermometer.

Salt the fish on both sides and pepper only on the under (skin) side. Put the fish in the hot oil, peppered side down, and cook until the fish is a little springy to the touch, 8 to 10 minutes. Be sure to maintain the oil at 180° to 190°F, adjusting the heat as necessary.

While the fish is cooking, make the sauce: Heat the remaining 2 table-spoons olive oil over medium-low heat in a sauté pan. Add the scallions and cook over low heat until soft, about 3 minutes. Add the garlic. Stir in half the shredded basil. Then add the tomatoes and vinegar, raise the heat to medium, and cook for another 2 minutes. Add the rest of the basil and season with salt and pepper to taste.

Spoon the sauce onto 4 hot plates and put the pieces of fish on top. Garnish with basil leaves or herb flowers.

Sautéed Flounder Fillets with Watercress Sauce

FRANK STITT

SERVES 6

1/2 cup	all-purpose flour
	salt and freshly ground pepper
6	flounder fillets, 6 to 8 ounces each
2 tablespoons	olive oil
1 tablespoon	unsalted butter
1 recipe	Watercress Gribiche (recipe follows)
2	lemons, quartered

Put the flour in a shallow pan or baking tray and season with salt and pepper. Dredge the fish in the seasoned flour to coat lightly on each side. Shake off any excess.

Heat the oil and butter in a large skillet over medium-high heat. When the butter stops foaming, add the flounder skin side up. Cook until pale golden on the bottom, about 3 minutes. Turn the fillets over and cook the fish until done, another 3 to 6 minutes depending on the thickness of the fillets.

Drain the fillets for a few seconds on paper towels, then put them on heated plates. Add a large spoon of watercress sauce and pass the rest on the side. Garnish with lemon quarters to squeeze over the fish.

Frank Stitt's stuffed flounder.

When I visited Frank, some wonderful hand line-caught, or "gigged," 2-pound flounders came in on the fish truck from Apalachicola. So we boned the fish and stuffed them with a mixture of chopped shrimp, crabmeat, watercress, lemon zest, chives, shallots, and Tabasco, all held together with buttered fresh white bread crumbs. They were the fish special that night at the Bar & Grill.

Of course, my favorite mayonnaise-based sauce, French *gribiche*, was served with it, and Frank's version is loaded with watercress. He serves the fish with black-eyed, or lady, peas and watercress dipped 30 seconds in boiling salted water and tossed in extra virgin olive oil.

Watercress Gribiche

1 bunch	watercress, washed, stemmed, leaves retained
1	egg yolk
3/4 cup	grapeseed or canola oil
1/2	lemon, juiced
1	small shallot, finely minced
1 tablespoon	capers, rinsed
1 tablespoon	cornichons, rinsed, chopped
6 leaves	fresh tarragon, finely chopped
1	hard-cooked egg, finely chopped
1 teaspoon	Dijon mustard
	salt and freshly ground white pepper

Parboil the watercress in boiling water for 10 seconds; drain, squeeze dry, and finely chop.

Whisk the egg yolk in a mixing bowl for 2 minutes. Slowly drizzle in the oil, still whisking.

Add the lemon juice, shallot, capers, cornichons, tarragon, cooked egg, mustard, and blanched watercress. Stir well. Season with salt and white pepper to taste.

Tip: This sauce needs to be made 2 hours (and up to overnight) before using so that the flavors combine and balance and you can do the final seasoning. But if holding it for more than 2 hours, add the cornichons at the end. They tend to disflavor the sauce after that.

Sautéed Squid
with Roasted Beet Salad

JEAN-MARIE LACROIX

SERVES 4

3	large red beets, stems trimmed to 1 inch
3 tablespoons	sherry vinegar
1/4 cup	extra virgin olive oil
	sugar
	sea salt and freshly ground pepper
2 tablespoons	olive oil
2 pounds	fresh young squid, cleaned, flattened, and cut into 2-inch squares

Preheat the oven to 350°F. Roast 2 of the beets until tender, about 1 hour. The beets can be roasted a day in advance.

When the beets are cool enough to handle, slip off the skins. Cut the beets into 1/8-inch-thick strips 2 inches long. Put the beet strips into a bowl and add 1 teaspoon of the vinegar, 2 tablespoons of the extra virgin olive oil, a pinch of sugar, and salt and pepper to taste. Arrange in a mound in the center of each of 4 large white plates.

Trim and peel the remaining beet and cut into 1-inch cubes. Put beet cubes in a food processor until coarsely pureed, about 2 minutes. Let the beet mixture sit for 10 minutes, then strain through a sieve into a small bowl; discard any beet remaining in the sieve. Stir in 1 teaspoon of the vinegar and the remaining 2 tablespoons extra virgin olive oil. Season with salt and pepper to taste. Set the beet vinaigrette aside.

Heat the olive oil in a frying pan large enough to hold all the squid in a single layer (or do in 2 batches). Season the squid and cook them in the hot oil over medium-high heat for about 30 seconds on each side. Do not be tempted to cook the squid longer, or it will become tough. Then pour the remaining vinegar into the pan and let it evaporate.

Arrange the squid squares around the beet salad. Pour some of the raw beet vinaigrette sauce around each plate.

SERVES 4

Ken uses jaune d'Arbois
wine in this dish. If you
cannot find it, use half the
quantity of the best rich,
but dry, sherry you can
buy. He uses sea beans as
part of the garnish.

Butter-Braised Lobster with Chanterelle and Fava Bean Stew

2 cups	water
2	lemons
1/2 pound plus 3 tablespoons	cold unsalted butter, cut into small pieces
	sea salt and freshly ground white pepper
2	Maine lobsters, 2 pounds each, cooked and cut up as described on page 194, coral reserved
1 recipe	Chanterelle and Fava Bean Stew (recipe follows)
1 cup	Lobster Stock (page 197)
	saffron threads
1 sprig	fresh tarragon
4 large sprigs	fresh chervil

Bring the water to a simmer, squeeze in the juice from the lemons, and then over medium heat whisk in $1/2$ pound of the butter in pieces until they are all incorporated into a smooth emulsion. Remove from the heat and season with salt and white pepper to taste.

Add the meat from the lobster tails and claws. Cook over the lowest possible heat, never letting the butter sauce get hotter than 160°F, for 20 minutes; if you are unsure of the temperature of your stove, cook for only 10 minutes; then remove from the heat and let the lobster sit in the butter sauce for another 10 minutes.

Meanwhile, make the chanterelle and fava bean stew.

Bring the lobster stock to a boil. Add a pinch of saffron and the tarragon, wait 2 minutes, then strain through a fine sieve over a bowl to remove the tarragon. Return the lobster stock to the saucepan and return to a boil. Put the lobster coral in a bowl. Remove the stock from the heat, wait 1 minute, and then whisk the cooling stock into the lobster coral. Do not let this sauce boil after this point, or it will curdle.

Whisk in the remaining 3 tablespoons cold butter and then $1/2$ cup of the buttery liquid in which the lobster meat is cooking. Season and keep hot but nowhere close to boiling.

Spoon the lobster coral sauce into 4 hot soup plates. Then add a spoon-ful of the chanterelle and fava bean stew, a lobster claw, and a lobster tail cut in half lengthwise, more chanterelles, a spoonful of the lobster cooking butter, and finally a sprig of chervil to each. Serve at once.

Chanterelle and Fava Bean Stew

SERVES 4

2 tablespoons	olive oil
1 cup	sliced chanterelles
2	large shallots, finely chopped
1/4 cup	jaune d'Arbois wine
1/2 cup	Rich Brown Chicken Stock (page 193)
2 tablespoons	finely chopped mixed fresh herbs: Italian parsley, chervil, tarragon, and chives
1 pound	fresh fava pods, beans removed and blanched for 1 to 2 minutes, peeled
1 tablespoon	hazelnut oil
	salt and freshly ground pepper

Put the olive oil in a large sauté pan and heat over medium heat. Add the chanterelles and stir for 2 minutes. Add the shallots and cook for another 2 minutes, or until softened. Pour in the wine and, when that is almost completely evaporated, add the chicken stock. Raise the heat a little and simmer until half the liquid is gone. Add the herbs, fava beans, and hazelnut oil. Cook for another 2 minutes. Season with salt and pepper to taste. Remove from the heat.

FRANK STITT

SERVES 6

At Frank's Highlands Bar & Grill, they sometimes use butternut squash instead of pumpkin, or a combination of both, in this dish. At the restaurant, they serve this with their Orange Hollandaise, but it's good even with just a drizzle of orange juice and extra virgin olive oil.

Pompano with Roasted Pumpkin, Vanilla Bean, and Grilled Lemon

1	small pie pumpkin or butternut squash, seeded, cut into 2$\frac{1}{2}$-inch chunks $\frac{1}{2}$ inch thick, skin cut off
1 tablespoon	unsalted butter, melted
	salt and freshly ground pepper
$\frac{1}{2}$	vanilla bean, split
6 fillets	fresh pompano, 6 ounces each, skin on
1 tablespoon	olive oil
2	lemons, cut into $\frac{1}{4}$-inch slices, seeded
1 recipe	Orange Hollandaise (recipe follows)
1 tablespoon	freshly grated orange zest
18 sprigs	parsley or chervil

Preheat the oven to 375°F.

Put the pumpkin chunks, melted butter, and salt and pepper in a baking pan or large gratin dish. Scrape the seeds of the vanilla bean half over the pumpkin. Throw the bean in, too, and toss until the pumpkin chunks are just coated. Bake for 20 minutes, or until the pumpkin is tender.

Preheat the grill or broiler.

Brush the pompano fillets with the olive oil and season with salt and pepper. Grill skin side up for 3 minutes. Turn the fish over and cook on the other side until done, 3 to 4 minutes, depending on the thickness of the fish.

Grill or broil the lemon slices until slightly charred.

Scatter the baked pumpkin and a couple of grilled lemon slices around each of 6 hot plates. Place the pompano in the center of the plates and drizzle hollandaise around the edges of the fish. Garnish the fish with the orange zest and 3 sprigs of the parsley or chervil.

Orange Hollandaise

1	orange
2 tablespoons	sugar
2	egg yolks
1 tablespoon	freshly squeezed orange juice
1/2 pound	unsalted butter (2 sticks), melted, kept warm
3 drops	Tabasco sauce
1	lemon, juiced
	salt

MAKES 1 CUP

Wash the orange and cut off the zest—only the orange skin, not the white pith—in 1/2- by 3-inch strips. Put the zest in a small saucepan with 1 cup water and bring to a boil. As soon as it boils, drain and discard the water. Repeat the same process. For the third parboiling, use 1/2 cup water and the 2 tablespoons sugar. After the water comes to a boil, cook for 5 minutes, remove from the heat, and let the zest cool in the sugar syrup.

Whisk the egg yolks in a medium stainless steel metal mixing bowl over a pot of simmering water until thickened and warm, about 5 minutes. Add the orange juice and continue whisking for another 2 minutes.

Start adding the butter slowly, whisking all the time, until the butter is used up. Add the Tabasco and lemon juice and season with salt to taste. Add enough of the strained orange-zest syrup to achieve the desired consistency.

SERVES 4

Charlie serves this rich dish with Brussels sprout leaves slow-cooked in olive oil and baby leeks braised in chicken stock.

Slow-Roasted Salmon with Coriander-Infused Chicken Liver Sauce

4 cups	Aromatic Vegetable Mix (page 207), made from leek, celery, ginger, thyme, parsley, and tarragon
4 pieces	fresh salmon fillet, skinned, 3 ounces each
	sea salt and freshly ground pepper
4 ounces	chicken livers, trimmed of all sinews
1 tablespoon	canola oil
1/4 cup	caramelized onions
1 teaspoon	coriander seeds, toasted
1/4 cup	dry red wine
1/2 cup	diced meaty bacon
1/2 cup	Brussels sprout leaves, preferably purple, parboiled
1/4 cup	diced, peeled Jerusalem artichokes (Sunchokes), boiled
2 tablespoons	champagne vinegar

Preheat the oven to 225°F.

Put the aromatic vegetable mix on a baking sheet and lay the pieces of salmon on top. Season the salmon with salt and pepper and put in the oven to slow-roast for about 25 minutes, until slightly translucent in the center.

While the salmon is cooking, make two sauces—the chicken liver sauce and a bacon vinaigrette. For the chicken liver sauce, heat the oil in a sauté pan. Season the livers with salt and pepper and add to the hot oil. Cook over medium heat for 1 minute, turn the livers over, and add the caramelized onions and the toasted coriander seeds. Continue to cook until the livers are still a bit pink on the inside, 3 to 5 minutes.

Pour in the red wine and bring to a boil, scraping up any brown bits from the bottom of the pan. Cook for 20 seconds and remove from the heat. Pour the contents of the pan into a blender or food processor and puree until smooth. Strain the liver sauce through a fine sieve into

Charlie Trotter's Slow-Roasted Salmon.

a small saucepan or double boiler. Keep warm but do not allow to come close to a boil, or the sauce will curdle.

For the bacon vinaigrette, cook the bacon in a large frying pan over medium-low heat until the bacon has rendered most of its fat, 8 to 10 minutes. Raise the heat to medium and add the Brussels sprout leaves, diced Jerusalem artichoke, and vinegar. Cook for 30 seconds, grind in some pepper, and keep warm.

To serve, spoon some of the chicken liver sauce around the outer edge of each of 4 hot plates. Put the vegetables in the center of the plate and the salmon pieces on top. Spoon the bacon vinaigrette over the salmon and around the plate, and grind some pepper over all.

(Above) Jeremiah in the kitchen with Nancy Oakes and her chef Pam Mazzola.

(Above) Making crab cakes. (Below) Jeremiah's oyster tartare.

JEREMIAH TALKS ABOUT

Nancy Oakes Boulevard Restaurant, San Francisco

THE MORNING I COOKED WITH NANCY OAKES FOR THIS BOOK was when I really started to know her. Up to that point I had met Nancy only at charity fund-raising events, and only then in a crowd of chefs all determined to pull off the impossible—great food in a tent or someone's parking lot for charity benefits. There I had seen those blue eyes fixed on the tasks at hand, but I had never seen them twinkle while looking—like a mother looking at beloved and well-behaved children—at perfect ingredients picked that morning by some-one she really liked. A friend had just walked into the Boulevard Restaurant kitchen with a basket of greens from her Berkeley garden that brought tears to my eyes even after all these years of tender lettuces, and a sigh of contentment from Nancy.

Other sighs could be heard coming from the dining room as diners settled into a décor that surrounds one in reassuring comfort while looking out onto the endless vista of the San Francisco Bay and its bridge. That, of course, is after you have sidled up to the bar for a perfect martini or glass of wine from Boulevard's list of California wines.

Like all the best chefs in America, Nancy's cooking is well sprung in the techniques, flavors, and satisfaction level of the past, both her personal one and the best of France, Italy, and America. But her cooking has a finely tuned, down-to-earth quality that is uniquely hers. As she said while basting the mushrooms nestled under the lamb chops cooking in the outdoor wood oven, "Isn't it great that after all these years we can still get excited about this stuff!"

When she presented the whole baked apples with streusel, her assessment was: "Homey, but still with a bit of style."

In her case, with a lot, and a lot of humor.

Those beautiful blue eyes challenged us to not believe that what lay beneath the humor was a love of cooking, of using perfect, locally grown ingredients, and of eating wonderful food shared with friends around the table.

America's Best Chefs Cook with Jeremiah Tower

Roasted Sea Bass
with Olives and Basil

NANCY OAKES

SERVES 6

6 fillets	California white sea bass, skin-on, about 6 ounces each, cut at least 1 inch thick
3 tablespoons	finely diced kalamata or other brine-cured black olives
1 teaspoon	finely diced Salt-Preserved Lemon (page 205)
3 tablespoons	Spoon's Pesto (page 38)
3 tablespoons	pure olive oil
	kosher salt and freshly ground pepper
1 recipe	Chunky Mashed Potatoes with Mascarpone and Arugula (page 140)
1 recipe	Grated Tomato Vinaigrette (recipe follows)

Cut 4 diagonal slices 1/2 inch deep into the flesh side of the fish. Mix together the olives and the preserved lemon. Stuff about 1/2 teaspoon of the mixture into every other cut. Stuff the basil pesto in the other 2 cuts.

Preheat the oven to 450°F.

Heat an ovenproof nonstick sauté pan large enough to hold all the fillets in one layer over medium heat. When hot, add the olive oil. Put the fish in the pan skin side up and reduce the heat to medium-low. Cook for 2 minutes, or until golden brown. Carefully turn the fillets over. Put the pan into the oven and roast for 4 minutes, or until the fish is cooked through (the cuts in the fish will cause it to cook more quickly). Season with salt and pepper to taste.

To serve, place a scoop of mashed potatoes on each of 6 warm dinner plates. Put a bass fillet on top, skin side up. Spoon the tomato vinaigrette around the plates.

As Nancy describes it, "This sea bass dish is the sort of food we [chefs] like to prepare when we want to make a good impression with a minimum of effort."

California white sea bass, the fish Nancy uses, is a medium-dense, moderately mild-flavored, lean fish. Other fish that could be substituted in this recipe are Atlantic grouper, drum, and mahi-mahi.

Nancy serves the fish with chunky mashed potatoes mixed with mascarpone and arugula (page 140). The fish can be stuffed, the tomato vinaigrette made, and the potatoes cooked (up until the point of combining them with the arugula and red pepper flakes) for reheating later in a microwave—all up to 6 hours in advance.

Grated Tomato Vinaigrette

This easy vinaigrette is also good on pasta, boiled vegetables—on just about anything that isn't a dessert. And it certainly helps the flavor if the tomatoes have never been refrigerated.

3	large vine-ripened red tomatoes (about 1 1/4 pounds)
1 tablespoon	balsamic vinegar
1/2 cup	extra virgin olive oil
1 teaspoon	kosher salt
	freshly ground pepper

Grate the tomatoes over a medium bowl as described in the tip below until only the skins remain. Discard the skins.

Mix in the vinegar and then slowly whisk in the olive oil until well combined. Season with the salt and pepper to taste. Set aside at room temperature for up to 6 hours.

Tip: A very quick, easy way to prepare skinned tomatoes for sauces is to grate them instead of using the boiling water dip, peel, and dice method. Cut very ripe tomatoes in half along their circumference and squeeze out the seeds. Grate the cut side on the large holes of a box grater. Voilà! Peeled, seeded, and diced.

People seem to think that chefs cook fabulously intricate and complex meals at home every night. Nothing could be further from the truth. We're as busy as everyone else and probably even less inclined to spend a great deal of time on dinner after standing in the kitchen all day.

—NANCY OAKES

America's Best Chefs Cook *with* Jeremiah Tower

Trout in Parchment with Crosnes, Fennel, Carrots, and Herbs

ODESSA PIPER

SERVES 4

4 fillets	trout, from 2 whole fish, boned
	sea salt and freshly ground pepper
1 cup	crosnes, scrubbed, or thickly sliced and peeled Jerusalem artichokes
1	large fennel bulb, cored and shaved into paper-thin slices
2	large carrots, cut into 1- by ⅛-inch sticks
¼ cup	cold-pressed grapeseed oil
1 tablespoon	fresh tarragon leaves, chopped
1 tablespoon	fresh chervil leaves, chopped
1 tablespoon	fresh Italian parsley leaves, chopped
1	lemon, preferably Meyer
¼ cup	herb shoots (lemon verbena, marjoram, or a mix; optional)

Preheat the oven to 400°F. Put the parchment (see text at right) on a baking sheet(s) and place 2 trout fillets on one circle of each parchment double round shape, with the belly or thin sides overlapping so that the 2 fillets have an even thickness. Season lightly with salt and pepper.

Continued

Odessa Piper's Trout in Parchment with Crosnes, Fennel, Carrots, and Herbs.

Odessa says that this is a March dish, because it uses the last of the root-cellar vegetables—in this case, crosnes. Crosnes look and taste like a bit of a cross between a Jerusalem artichoke and a small fingerling potato, despite the fact that they belong botanically to the mint family. They are very popular in France. If you can't find them here, substitute slices of Jerusalem artichoke.

The trout Odessa uses at her restaurant, Etoile, in Madison, Wisconsin, are from the cold waters of the glacial aquifer that feeds the springs at Artesian Farm, so the flesh is firm and pure. The other special ingredient here for Odessa is the organic, cold-pressed grapeseed oil, whose flavor is delicate enough for the trout.

To make the paper forms for this dish, use a large sheet of parchment on which you have drawn a solid figure-8, so that you have cut out 2 circular halves attached at the center where the circles meet, each circle a few inches longer than the filets of trout, or at least 15 inches.

In a large pot of salted boiling water, boil the crosnes, fennel, and carrots together for 1 minute. Drain, cool in a bowl of ice water, and drain well. Pack the crosnes, fennel, and carrots tightly around the edges of the fillets and season the vegetables with salt and pepper.

Mix half the grapeseed oil with the chopped herbs and spoon over the fish and the vegetables. Squeeze half the juice from the lemon over the fish.

Fold the other circle of parchment over the trout packages and, starting at one end of the connection, fold over the edges 3 times to crimp very tightly in a 1/2-inch fold all the way around the circle.

Bake for 7 to 10 minutes, depending on how cold the fish was. The parchment should puff up. Remove the parchment packets to a platter and open up in front of your guests with scissors. Fold back the parchment and scatter the herb shoots over the fish. Drizzle on the rest of the grapeseed oil and lemon juice, and pass the sea salt.

Olive Oil–Cooked Tuna with Lobster and Caviar

1 tablespoon	freshly squeezed lemon juice
1 teaspoon	champagne vinegar
1/4 cup	Lobster Stock (page 197)
	freshly ground white pepper
1/4 cup	olive oil from the tuna
1 recipe	Olive Oil–Cooked Tuna (recipe follows)
	meat from 1 cooked lobster (page 194)
1 ounce	sevruga caviar

To make the sauce, whisk together the lemon juice, vinegar, lobster stock, and a pinch of white pepper. Add the olive oil and stir briefly without emulsifying.

To serve, put the pieces of tuna on 4 plates. Place the lobster meat on top of the tuna and top with a small dollop of caviar. Spoon the sauce equally over any uncovered tuna and around the plate.

JEREMIAH TOWER

SERVES 4

The list of ingredients may look long for the preparation of the tuna, but the beauty is that you can prepare the fish up to 2 weeks in advance. While I offer a different presentation here, you can use the tuna on open-faced sandwiches, in salads, or however you want.

Prepare the Olive Oil–Cooked Tuna as described in the recipe that follows. For cooking the tuna, you will need four 1-pint canning

America's Best Chefs Cook *with* Jeremiah Tower

Olive Oil–Cooked Tuna

¼ cup	black peppercorns, toasted
1 tablespoon	sea salt
4 pieces	fresh fatty tuna, 6 to 8 ounces each, cut 3 inches thick
8	salted anchovy fillets (page 96)
4 sprigs	fresh thyme
4 leaves	fresh sage
8 sprigs	Italian parsley
1 tablespoon	fresh rosemary leaves
4	bay leaves
8 cloves	garlic, crushed
2 tablespoons	freshly grated lemon zest
4 cups	extra virgin olive oil

Grind the black peppercorns and salt together and rub over the pieces of tuna. Let sit for 30 minutes. Then wipe off half any marinade sticking to the fish.

Put an anchovy fillet in the bottom of each of four 1-pint canning jars. Then add half the thyme, sage, parsley, rosemary, bay leaves, and garlic, dividing the ingredients equally among the 4 jars. Place a piece of tuna in each jar, then add the lemon zest. Divide the remaining herbs and anchovy fillets equally on top of each piece of tuna and pour enough of the olive oil over each piece of tuna to cover it by at least ½ inch.

Close the jars and put them in a water bath with the water coming up to the necks of the jars. Cover and simmer very gently for 2 hours. Test to see if the fish is tender (timing will depend on the kind of tuna) and cook longer if necessary. Let cool before serving. If this recipe is made ahead of time, refrigerate for up to 2 weeks and serve at room temperature.

jars. If made ahead, let the tuna return to room temperature. Cook the lobster as described on page 194, or purchase a cooked lobster. Remove the lobster meat from the shells and cut it into 2-inch medallions.

If you happen to have some lobster-shellfish stock in the freezer, and a bit of leftover lobster meat and caviar on hand, this dish is 10 minutes away from the table. I hate the word *optional* in recipes, but in this case, the caviar really is.

SERVES 4

At the Heathman restaurant in Portland, Oregon, Philippe serves this tuna dish with potatoes *dauphine*, which are mashed potatoes mixed with choux paste (milk, butter, flour, and eggs), formed into little quenelle shapes with two spoons, and then deep fried. They puff up light as a feather and taste delicious. If you prefer a less time-consuming accompaniment, simply boil some Yukon gold or fingerling potatoes and toss them with butter and parsley.

Do not give up this dish if you don't have truffles. It is, I dare say, excellent without any sauce at all.

Philppe Boulot's shopping list.

Tuna Medallions with Foie Gras and Truffle Sauce

4 pieces	fresh tuna, about 6 ounces each
4 slices	raw duck or goose liver (foie gras), about 2 ounces each
	sea salt and freshly ground pepper
2 tablespoons	olive oil
2 cups	blanched and squeezed-dry spinach
4 tablespoons	unsalted butter
4 slices	brioche or Challah bread, crusts removed, each 1/4-inch thick and 2 1/2 inches square
1 recipe	Oregon Black Truffle Sauce (recipe follows)

Season the tuna steak and foie gras slices with salt and pepper.

Heat the olive oil in a sauté pan until quite hot. Sear the tuna over medium-high heat, cooking for 2 to 3 minutes on each side, depending on how thick the tuna pieces are. The fish should be warm at the center but still rare. Set aside and keep warm.

Meanwhile, heat the spinach with the butter. Season with salt and pepper to taste.

As soon as the tuna is done, tip the oil out of the pan. Add the foie gras and sear and cook 30 seconds or so on each side, until medium-rare. Set aside the tuna and foie gras and keep warm while you cook the brioche.

In the same pan with the fat rendered from the foie gras, fry the brioche over medium heat for 30 seconds on each side, until lightly browned.

Put the toasted brioche pieces on 4 hot plates. Then put the tuna on top of the brioche and the foie gras on top of the tuna. Put 3 little piles of the spinach equidistant around the toasts. Pour the Oregon truffle sauce over the foie gras at the table.

Oregon Black Truffle Sauce

6	large shallots, peeled, minced finely
1 cup	malmsey Madeira
1 sprig	fresh thyme
1 cup	Meat Jus (page 201) or storebought
1	Oregon fresh black truffle, chopped
1 tablespoon	unsalted butter
1 drop	freshly squeezed lemon juice
	sea salt

MAKES 1 1/2 CUPS

Sweat the shallots in a covered 1-quart saucepan with 2 tablespoons of water until they are soft, about 5 minutes. Add the Madeira and the thyme and simmer, uncovered, until reduced by half. Add the meat jus and cook for another 2 minutes. Strain, discarding the shallots and thyme.

Return to the same pan and boil until the sauce is reduced by one quarter and has a nice consistency. Add the truffle and cook for 1 minute. Whisk in the butter and lemon juice. Season with salt.

PATRICK O'CONNELL

SERVES 4

Filet Mignon of Rare Tuna with Foie Gras

Here a center-cut portion of tuna is trimmed to resemble a filet mignon of beef grilled rare, topped with a slab of seared, fattened duck liver (foie gras) and sauced with an explosively full-flavored red wine sauce. It's served resting on charred onions and ribbons of zucchini and carrot. Naturally, the same concept works beautifully with a filet of beef. Make tuna cakes or tartare from any tuna trimmings.

1	very large white onion, cut into $1/4$-inch-thick slices
1/4 cup	olive oil
2	large carrots, sliced lengthwise into paper-thin, wide ribbons
2	medium zucchini, sliced lengthwise into paper-thin, wide ribbons
	sea salt and freshly ground pepper
2 tablespoons	hot Brown Butter (page 202)
4	center-cut tuna steaks, 6 ounces each, trimmed to the shape of a filet mignon
1/4 cup	extra virgin olive oil
4 ounces	raw fattened duck liver (foie gras), cut in 4 slices $1/2$ inch thick, chilled
1 recipe	Burgundy Butter Sauce (recipe follows)

Heat a cast-iron ridged grill pan over high heat until very hot. Moisten the onion slices with the olive oil and place them in a single layer on the hot pan. Cook until lightly charred, 3 to 5 minutes. Turn over with tongs and char the other side. Repeat until all the slices are cooked. Set aside.

Meanwhile, bring 2 quarts of lightly salted water to a rapid boil and drop in the carrot ribbons. Cook 1 to 2 minutes, or until the carrots are tender but still al dente. Lift the ribbons out with a slotted spoon and place in a bowl. Repeat the same cooking process with the zucchini ribbons, remembering that they will cook much faster than the carrots. Add the drained zucchini to the carrots, season them with salt and pepper, and mix gently with the hot brown butter. Keep warm.

Moisten the tuna steaks with the olive oil and season with salt and pepper. Put them on a hot charcoal grill or onto the same grill pan used to char the onions. Sear the tuna 2 minutes on each side and keep hot.

Season the slices of foie gras with salt and pepper and season on both sides in a smoking-hot medium sauté pan for 30 seconds on each side, or until a crisp outer crust just forms on the liver. Remove and keep warm.

America's Best Chefs Cook *with* Jeremiah Tower

Lay 3 or 4 charred onion rings in the center of each of 4 hot serving plates. Arrange 2 ribbons of carrots and 2 of zucchini over the onions in a circular nestlike pattern. Place the hot tuna steaks on top and arrange the foie gras on top of the tuna steaks, followed by more onions. Sauce the plate with 3 pools of the Burgundy Butter Sauce and serve at once.

Burgundy Butter Sauce

1 cup	plus 2 tablespoons red wine
1	shallot, peeled, cut in half
1 cup	balsamic vinegar
4 tablespoons	cold *unsalted* butter, cut into 4 pieces
8 tablespoons	cold *salted* butter (1 stick), cut into 8 pieces
	salt and freshly ground pepper

MAKES 1 CUP

Patrick uses this on his Filet Mignon of Rare Tuna with Foie Gras but it is wonderful also on any poached or grilled fish, as well as on poached eggs and chicken breasts.

Combine the red wine, shallot, and vinegar in a nonreactive heavy saucepan and simmer over low heat until reduced to a syrupy consistency.

Slowly incorporate the cold butter into the sauce while simmering, stirring with a wooden spoon and adding one piece of butter at a time; add the next piece when the previous one has just melted into the sauce.

Remove the shallot and season the sauce. Keep warm until needed.

Tuna lends itself very well to some of the same methods of cooking as beef. This preparation could confuse a blindfolded cowboy into thinking he was biting into a succulent steak.
—*PATRICK O'CONNELL*

Swordfish Steak au Poivre with Lily Bulb and Pomelo Salad

SERVES 4

Having dinner at Ken Oringer's Clio in Boston the night before I cooked with him on the beach at Scituate, Massachusetts, I found a leaf in a salad that was new to me. I was told it was lily bulb. The next morning I walked over to the Asian market that Ken suggested and found the bulbs. It turns out that they are commonly sold in Chinese markets sealed in plastic, but if you can't find them, use sliced fresh water chestnuts mixed with chopped Belgian endive.

Before heading to the kitchen, I also picked up some fresh young ginger and some tiny dried shrimp from Vietnam. I had no idea what I was going to do with the ingredients, but after I found some perfect pink swordfish, I put this dish together.

2 tablespoons	black peppercorns
2 tablespoons	white peppercorns
4	swordfish steaks, 4 to 6 ounces each
1/4 cup	olive oil
	sea salt
1 pound	fresh lily bulbs, cored, leaves removed
1/4 cup	organic cold-pressed canola or peanut oil
1 tablespoon	fresh young ginger, preferably Hawaiian, peeled, finely chopped
1/2 tablespoon	crystallized ginger, finely chopped
2 tablespoons	tiny dried shrimp, cooked 10 seconds in vegetable oil, drained, chopped
	zest and juice from 2 limes
1	ripe pomelo, sections cut out of the fruit and its compartments
2 tablespoons	extra virgin olive oil

Preheat the oven to 400°F.

Toast the peppercorns in a dry wok or large skillet over medium heat, stirring often, until fragrant, about 1 minute. Put the peppercorns in a small baking dish and crush them with the bottom of a saucepan. Put the pepper through a fine sieve, saving the dust that falls through separately from the coarse pieces of pepper.

Dip the swordfish steaks in the olive oil on both sides and then press into the coarse pepper. Salt the fish.

Heat a large, dry seasoned cast-iron skillet and cook the swordfish for 2 minutes on each side. Transfer the skillet to the oven and bake for 5 minutes. Remove the pan and let sit for another 5 minutes, or less if the fish is done; it should remain translucent in the very center.

Jeremiah's Swordfish Steak au Poivre with Lily Bulb and Pomelo Salad.

Meanwhile, put the lily bulb leaves, canola oil, fresh and crystallized ginger, dried shrimp, half the lime juice, and a pinch each of salt and fine pepper in a bowl. Toss to mix the salad. When you take the fish out of the oven, put the salad in a large frying pan and heat over medium heat, tossing constantly, for 2 minutes, just to warm it through. Remove from the heat, add the pomelo sections, and toss again.

Divide the salad among 4 warm plates. Put the fish on top and drizzle with the olive oil and remaining lime juice. Sprinkle the lime zest and some of the reserved fine pepper powder on top and serve.

Sole Normande

SERVES 4 TO 6

1½ pounds	fresh sole fillets, preferably Petrale sole, 2 to 3 ounces each
2	shallots, finely chopped
1 cup	unsweetened French cider or dry white wine, preferably sauvignon blanc
2 cups	heavy cream
	salt and freshly ground white pepper
¼ pound	mushrooms, sliced thinly
2 tablespoons	unsalted butter

This dish has nothing—and everything—to do with Normandy. The conundrum lies in the fact that the classic garnish, *"a la normande,"* contains oysters, mussels, and shrimp—so far so good, as far as Normandy is concerned. The puzzle starts when the list continues: mushrooms, shredded fresh black truffles, freshwater crayfish cooked in vegetable broth, fried gudgeon (small fish), and shaped croutons. That is obviously the cooking of the Ile de France and its *grande cuisine* capital, Paris.

Philippe has wisely stuck to the original, much simpler concept: fish stewed in the heavenly fresh thick cream of Normandy along with its cider. Serve with buttered fingerling potatoes tossed with haricots verts.

Pound the fillets gently with the flat side of a knife to tenderize them slightly.

Put the shallots and cider or wine in a large sauté pan and bring to a boil. Reduce the heat to a simmer and cook for another 2 minutes. Add the cream.

Season the fish fillets with salt and white pepper on the skinned side and fold over end to end. Put the folded fish into the cream. Cover and cook over very low heat until the fish is firm, about 5 minutes.

Philippe Boulot's Sole Normande.

Add the mushrooms, cover again, and cook for 3 minutes. Carefully remove the fish and mushrooms from the pan; cover to keep warm. Boil the cream until it is reduced by half, or until it lightly coats a spoon.

Drain any juices from the fish and mushrooms into the sauce. Season with salt and white pepper to taste. Return the sauce to a boil. Remove from the heat and whisk in the butter. Gently return the fish and mushrooms to the hot sauce and let sit 3 minutes to reheat before serving.

Salted Anchovies

I have never failed to convert an anchovy hater into a devotee after I introduced them to salted anchovies. Banish all those tins of oil-packed anchovy filets. Buy a can or jar of salted ones—the jar is usually round and looks like a lot more anchovies than you need. It isn't.

Open the can and scrape off the top layer of salt; keep it for topping off the remaining anchovies. Lift out the dozen little fish you are going to use and brush off the salt gently. Take all the other fish out of the can and put them in a glass canning jar or plastic container with a lid. Put all the salt back on top of the fish, cover, and store in the refrigerator for up to 3 months until needed again.

Holding each fish belly side up under cold running water (with not too much pressure), slit open the cavity with your thumbnail. Open up the fish along the backbone, then remove and discard the bone. Rinse each fillet (two per fish) under the water, remove and discard the little dorsal fin, and put the fillets on a plate. Repeat until all the fish are cleaned and filleted.

Then, and only then, put the fillets together in a bowl of cold water to soak away some of the saltiness. Leave for 10 minutes, drain, and repeat. Drain gently and lay out on paper towels. Gather the anchovy fillets up and put them in a little bowl with extra virgin olive oil, just enough to cover them by 1/4 inch.

Leave the fillets in the oil for a few hours. Then they are ready to use on salads (like Caesar) or with roasted bell peppers. Or blend them into butter with fresh tarragon and put on top of a baked potato. Or just put the fish on garlic bread with lots of black pepper and eat as a snack. You will never go near another oil-packed anchovy again.

Poultry, Rabbit,
and Foie Gras

SERVES 4 TO 6

Ducasse serves this chicken on toasted country bread, sauced only with a rich chicken stock deglazing of the roasting pan and garnished with mixed garden vegetables.

Chicken Roasted with Herbs Stuffed Under the Skin

10 ounces	unsalted butter (2^1/2 sticks), at cool room temperature
1 bunch	flat-leaf parsley
1 bunch	fresh chervil
1 sprig	fresh tarragon, stemmed
^{1}/2 pound	white button mushrooms, finely chopped
	salt and freshly ground pepper
1	shallot, thinly sliced
1	large roasting chicken, about 5 pounds
4 cups	Rich Brown Chicken Stock (page 193)

To make the herb butter, put 1 stick plus 6 tablespoons of the butter in a bowl and beat it with a spoon (or do this in a mixer) until smooth and creamy. Chop 3/4 of the parsley and chervil leaves and all of the tarragon and blend with the butter. Save the remaining parsley and chervil sprigs for garnishing the plates.

Cook the chopped mushrooms in the remaining 6 tablespoons butter in a sauté pan over medium heat until soft, about 6 minutes. Season with salt and pepper, remove from the heat, and let cool. Add the cooled mushrooms and the shallot slices to the herb butter and mix thoroughly.

Preheat the oven to 350°F. Starting at the back end of the chicken breast, slip your fingers under the skin and carefully lift it from the flesh of the chicken without tearing it. When both sides of the breast have been separated, spread the herb butter evenly between the skin and the flesh of the breast meat. Pull the skin back over the breast.

Either spit-roast or bake the chicken in the oven for 45 minutes. Pour the chicken stock over the chicken and roast, basting occasionally with the pan juices, for 45 minutes longer, or until the thigh juices run clear when pierced near the bone.

Let the chicken rest for about 10 minutes. Skim the fat off the pan juices. Carve the chicken and serve with the pan juices.

Chicken Saltimbocca

MICHAEL ROMANO

SERVES 4

4	organic, free-range fresh skinless, boneless chicken breast halves, about 6 ounces each
	sea salt and freshly ground pepper
12	large fresh sage leaves, stemmed
6 thin slices	prosciutto, cut crosswise in half
1 cup	all-purpose flour
1/2 cup	freshly grated Pecorino Romano cheese
4	large eggs
1/2 cup plus 2 tablespoons	extra virgin olive oil
1 recipe	Sautéed Spinach with Garlic (page 145)
	lemon wedges

Saltimbocca, or "jump in your mouth," is more like "jump right off the prep table into the pan and into your mouth in 20 minutes." This is a delicious, easy-to-prepare dish, which can be made with pork, turkey, or veal as well as chicken. It is also fast to cook and can be finished right in front of your guests.

Michael dips the chicken first into flour mixed with cheese and then into egg beaten with a little oil, which makes a delicate, light coating. He serves the saltimbocca sauceless except for some juice squeezed out of a ripe lemon and accompanies it with spinach cooked in olive oil with garlic (page 145).

Slice each piece of chicken breast crosswise into 3 equal pieces. Spread a fingertip of cold water over each piece, put the pieces between sheets of heavy-duty plastic wrap, and pound out with a mallet until 1/4 inch thick.

Lightly season the pieces of chicken with salt and pepper. Place a sage leaf and a slice of prosciutto on each, pressing the prosciutto into the chicken. Mix the flour and Pecorino cheese together. Beat the eggs with the 2 tablespoons of the olive oil in a shallow bowl.

Heat the remaining 1/2 cup oil in a large sauté pan over medium-high heat. Dip the saltimbocca pieces into the flour and cheese; shake off any excess. Then dip into the egg mixture and put them into the hot oil. Cook for 2 minutes on each side.

Serve the saltimbocca with the Sautéed Spinach with Garlic and lemon wedges to squeeze over the chicken.

Tip: A drop of water spread on the chicken before pounding it out makes the job easier and faster.

Michael Romano's Chicken Saltimbocca.

FRANK STITT

SERVES 4 TO 6

Braised Guinea Hen with Wild Mushrooms and Country Ham

One of the best lunches I ever had was by myself on a wet, blustery summer Sunday afternoon on the coast of Brittany. After pristine Belon oysters, I had a roast guinea hen, accompanied by French fries and a watercress salad. For years I have tried in vain to duplicate that simple roast fowl, but Frank is right: guinea fowl raised in America should be braised rather than roasted.

This same recipe also works well with free-range natural chickens. He serves both with the vegetables on page 142.

2	fresh guinea hens, about 2 pounds each
1 clove	garlic, crushed
1/2	onion, thinly sliced
1 tablespoon	olive oil
1 tablespoon	each fresh thyme, marjoram, winter savory leaves
	sea salt and freshly ground pepper
2 tablespoons	vegetable oil
1 cup	Aromatic Vegetable Mix (page 207)
2 cups	dry red wine
2 tablespoons	ruby port
1 tablespoon	dried porcini mushrooms (cepes, boletus)
1 sprig	fresh thyme
1	bay leaf
3 cups	chicken stock
1 piece	ham bone, rind, or slice from shank
4 tablespoons	unsalted butter
2 cups	fresh chanterelles or other wild mushrooms, sliced
2 thin slices	southern-style country ham or Smithfield ham, cut into very thin strips 2 inches long

Cut each guinea hen into serving pieces: Remove the legs and thighs and separate them. Remove the wing, just above the ball and socket joint. Split the breast and cut side crosswise. Put all the pieces in a bowl. Add the garlic, onion, olive oil, and herbs; toss to coat lightly. Let marinate at room temperature for 30 minutes, tossing once.

Preheat the oven to 375°F.

Remove the guinea hen pieces from the marinade and pat dry; reserve the marinade. Season the pieces of guinea hen with salt and pepper. Heat the vegetable oil in a heavy skillet or cast-iron casserole. When hot, sear the pieces of guinea hen over medium-high heat until golden brown on both sides. Remove and place on a cooling rack set over a cookie sheet. Put the vegetable mix and marinade ingredients in the skillet and cook for 15 minutes over medium heat, stirring often, until they are lightly browned.

America's Best Chefs Cook *with* Jeremiah Tower

Pour in the red wine and port and bring to a boil. Cook until reduced to about 1/3 cup. Add the porcini, thyme, bay leaf, and chicken stock. Bring to a simmer and cook for 3 minutes.

Put the pieces of guinea hen and the ham bone in a gratin dish just large enough to hold them and the vegetables. Pour the vegetables and their liquid over the guinea hen. Cover with foil and place in the oven. Reduce the oven temperature to 325°F and braise for 15 minutes.

Test the breast pieces for doneness and remove them when cooked. Continue to cook the remaining pieces. When all the guinea hen is done, return the breast meat to the gratin dish. Strain the braising liquid into a saucepan; discard the vegetables and ham bone. Boil until the liquid is reduced by half. Taste and adjust the seasoning. Pour the sauce over the pieces in the gratin dish.

Heat 2 tablespoons of the butter in a large sauté pan and add the chanterelles. Season with salt and pepper. Cook over medium heat, stirring, for 5 minutes.

Heat the gratin dish until the guinea hen is hot, swirl in the remaining butter, and serve with the chanterelles. Scatter the strips of ham over the guinea hen and serve.

Grilled Duck Breasts with Green Chile Macaroni

4	whole fresh boneless duck breasts
2 tablespoons	Roaring Fork Dry Chili Salt Cure (recipe follows)
1 recipe	Red Bell Pepper Sauce (page 202)
1/4 cup	canola oil
1 recipe	Green Chile Macaroni (page 60)
1 recipe	Chow-Chow (recipe follows)

Score the skin of the duck breasts 1/8 inch deep and rub them with the dry chili salt cure.

Mix the pepper sauce with the canola oil and cook in a small saucepan over low heat, stirring often, until reduced to a ketchup, about 20 minutes. Keep warm.

Continued

ROBERT MCGRATH

SERVES 4

At his Roaring Fork restaurant, Robert serves this dish with a red bell pepper sauce on the plate under the duck and the chow-chow relish sprinkled over the sliced duck.

Grill the duck breasts over a hot wood or charcoal fire or under a pre-heated broiler, starting with the fat side against the heat. Cook them 3/4 of the way through on that side before turning them over. Cook until just still pink or medium-rare. Let rest for 5 minutes. Carve crosswise on an angle into slices.

To serve, drizzle the warm bell pepper sauce in a circle in the center of each of 4 hot plates. Put the slices of duck breast on top and sprinkle with the chow-chow.

Roaring Fork's Dry Chili Salt Cure for Meats

6	dried ancho chilies, toasted in a skillet or over a fire
2/3 cup	kosher salt
1/4 cup	sugar
1 tablespoon	freshly ground pepper

MAKES 1 CUP

While this is one recipe for Robert McGraths's salt cure, he emphasizes that you should play around with the proportions and ingredients to suit your own adventurous tastes.

Stem and seed the ancho chilies. Grind them in an electric spice grinder, sieve, and mix with the salt, sugar, and pepper. Use as soon as possible, or store in a closed jar in a cool place for up to 2 weeks.

Chow-Chow

2	fresh red poblano peppers, stemmed, seeded, finely diced
1	large white onion, finely diced
1 tablespoon	mixed pickling spice
1/2 cup	rice vinegar
	salt

MAKES ABOUT 1 CUP

This relish is even better if made a day in advance.

Mix the red poblanos with the onion in a nonreactive saucepan. Add the pickling spice and vinegar and cook until the vegetables are soft, 10 minutes. Season with salt and let sit for at least 1 hour at room temperature, or cover and refrigerate for a day. Drain before using.

America's Best Chefs Cook *with* Jeremiah Tower

Foie Gras au Torchon

PHILIPPE BOULOT

SERVES 6 TO 8

1	whole fresh foie gras, about 1 1/2 pounds, nerves and ligaments removed
1 tablespoon	apple or pear eau-de-vie
	sea salt and freshly ground pepper
1 quart	rendered duck fat (page 209)
1 cup	apple cider
1 tablespoon	apple cider vinegar
1 teaspoon	Calvados
1/3 cup	hazelnut oil
1/2 cup	finely diced apple
2 bunches	mache or lambs' lettuce, rinsed, spun dry
1 loaf	brioche, crust removed, cut into slices 1/2 inch thick

The *torchon* is a foie gras rolled up and compressed into a sausage shape 2 to 3 inches in diameter, then cooked, cooled, and cured. It is served slightly chilled, usually on toast—here, with brioche.

You will need a clean kitchen towel. Keep in mind when planning that this preparation takes 3 days.

Wet a clean kitchen towel and wring out until just damp. Put the liver in the center toward one long edge of the towel. Sprinkle the foie gras with the eau-de-vie, salt, and pepper. Roll up the towel and shape it evenly and tightly into a sausage 2 to 3 inches in diameter. Twist the ends of the towel in opposite directions and tie the ends off with string, making sure there is no slack. Refrigerate overnight.

Put the duck fat in an oval flameproof casserole or fish poacher just large enough to hold the torchon and the fat. Bring the fat to a simmer, turn down the heat to very low, and when the fat is 165°F, put the *torchon* (towel and all) in the casserole with the fat. Let cook for 10 minutes, turning. Remove from the heat, let cool for 15 minutes, and then refrigerate the *torchon* in the fat for 2 days. When ready to use, unwrap the liver. Cut into 1-inch-thick rounds.

Boil the apple cider until reduced to 1/4 cup; let cool slightly. Put the vinegar, reduced cider, and Calvados in a small bowl. Add salt and pepper and whisk until the salt dissolves. Whisk in the hazelnut oil, then stir the apples into the dressing.

Toss the mache with the apple dressing. Put a round of liver on each round of brioche and serve with the dressed salad to the side.

Frank Stitt and Jeremiah on the front steps of Frank's house in Birmingham, Alabama.

JEREMIAH TALKS ABOUT

Frank Stitt Highlands Bar & Grill, Birmingham, Alabama

THE FIRST TIME I WALKED INTO THE HIGHLANDS BAR & GRILL IN BIRMINGHAM, Alabama, I found Frank Stitt at a tasting of great white Burgundies, overseeing the beginning of the regular Tuesday night martini fests and explaining one of the new dishes for the evening to the staff. Well, I thought, if great wines, martinis, and Gulf flounder stuffed with line-caught (gigged) blue crab are part of the American Southeast region, I had come to a place after my own heart.

I cannot think of any chef who is more true to the traditions of his region, with his love of France and Italy thrown in for good measure, than Frank.

"It's about that love of the land, of humble ingredients . . . working with seasonal ingredients and local traditions," he said to me while we were cooking at his house for a group of friends. He talked about his grandparents' farm, and how the table was always groaning with bowls upon bowls of what they had picked from the garden and cooked. He spoke of how there was always another place set at the table in case someone arrived unexpectedly, and offered that you did not have to be rich to have a rich family life enhanced by a strong sense of place.

The next day Frank and his wife, Pardis, showed me around his restaurants. I could see that they had taken that sense of family hospitality and its plentiful good food and translated it into a kind of restaurant hospitality that made their customers feel as if they were part of a larger family. What struck me the most was the feeling of propriety that all the regulars had: they knew as much about Frank, the restaurants, and what was going on as would any publicist, and they found great pleasure in telling me all they knew. At the Highlands Martini Night, the bar customers who had been attending those nights and eating in the restaurant for years held my attention for hours with interesting stories from

America's Best Chefs Cook *with* Jeremiah Tower

the opening night to five minutes earlier. At Frank's French bistro Fonfon and Italian Bottega, the diners were discussing not local events, but events that were coming up in Frank's restaurants. Of course, each diner had his or her opinion of which was going to be the best, and which of the restaurants was the best.

Many restaurateurs talk about the sense of place within the civic community that they try to make with their operation, but I have never seen restaurants as fiercely guarded and loved as Frank Stitt's. The impression I came away with was one of a very well-mannered and civilized community. The diners at Highlands said a great deal of that achievement was because of Frank.

(Above) A splendid table set in Frank Stitt's dining room.
(Below left) Frank and Jeremiah getting ready for the cameras.

Louisiana Rabbit with Wild Mushrooms and Spoonbread

Marinade

1	onion, sliced
3 cloves	garlic, crushed
2 sprigs	each fresh rosemary and thyme
1/4 cup	olive oil
4	juniper berries, crushed
1 cup	rich red wine, Syrah or Côtes du Rhone
2	fresh rabbits, cut into serving portions (legs, thighs, half-rib, etc.)

Braising ingredients

1/2 cup	dried porcini mushrooms (cepes, boletus)
1/2 cup	chicken stock
	salt and freshly ground pepper
1/2 cup	all-purpose flour
1/4 cup	olive oil
2	carrots, diced
2 cloves	garlic, minced
2 cups	rich red wine, Syrah or Côtes du Rhone
1/2 cup	ruby port
4 sprigs	fresh thyme tied up with 6 stems fresh parsley, leek tops, and 2 bay leaves to make an herb bundle
1/4 pound	fresh porcini, morel, chanterelles, or cremini mushrooms
3 tablespoons	butter
2 tablespoons	chopped mixed fresh parsley and basil leaves
1 recipe	Spoonbread (page 63)

Mix all the marinade ingredients in a bowl large enough to hold them and the pieces of rabbit. Add the rabbit and mix well with your hands until all the pieces are covered in marinade. Let sit 15 minutes, mix again, and let marinate another 1 1/2 hours, mixing once more.

Put the dried mushrooms in the chicken stock to steep for 30 minutes.

Frank Stitt's Louisiana Rabbit with Wild Mushrooms and Spoonbread.

Remove the pieces of rabbit from the marinade and set the marinade aside. Dry the rabbit pieces with paper towels, season with salt and pepper, and dust with the flour.

Heat the olive oil in a heavy skillet with a heatproof handle or a cast-iron casserole. Sear the rabbit pieces in a single layer with 1 inch between the pieces so that they don't steam from overcrowding and the oil doesn't burn from not having enough pieces in the skillet. When lightly browned on one side, turn the pieces over and brown on the other. Remove the pieces and put them on a wire cooling rack set on a baking sheet.

Preheat the oven to 325°F.

Strain the marinade over a bowl to collect the liquid. Add the carrots and minced garlic, and the onion, garlic, and herbs from the marinade to the skillet. Cook over medium heat, stirring occasionally, until soft, about 10 minutes. Add the dried mushrooms and their liquid. Bring to a boil, then add the marinade wine and the other red wine and port. Return to a boil and skim off all surface scum and fat.

Lower the heat until the liquid stops simmering. Add the rabbit pieces and herb bundle. Return to a simmer, cover, and transfer to the oven.

Continued

Poultry, Rabbit, and Foie Gras

Louisiana Rabbit with Wild Mushrooms, ready to plate.

Cook for 15 minutes. Remove the loin (back) pieces, cover again, and continue braising until the legs are cooked, about another 30 minutes.

Remove all the rabbit pieces. Strain the braising liquid and put the braising vegetables through a sieve or food mill; return to the liquid. Boil the sauce over medium heat, skimming again, for 15 minutes. Season with salt and pepper to taste. Add the rabbit to the sauce and gently reheat.

Sauté the fresh mushrooms in the butter in a large skillet over medium-high heat for 1 minute. Season with salt and pepper and continue cooking until some of their juices are extruded but the mushrooms are still firm, 3 to 5 minutes.

Serve the rabbit and its sauce with the mushrooms (and their juices) in the center. Garnish the dish with the chopped parsley and basil. Pass the spoonbread on the side.

Meats

ALAIN DUCASSE

SERVES 4

In Ducasse's wonderful book written with Linda Dannenberg, *The Flavors of France,* this dish was given the grand title of *Piece de Boeuf de Chalosse Poêle en Croute de Poivre, Grosses Frites a la Graise d'Oie, et Salade Croquante de Coeurs de Laitue.* To us, it's "steak au poivre." What caught my eye were the potatoes—fat French fries cooked in goose fat—the most sublime way to cook them, if not using rendered beef suet the way the English used to do. Try them once, and if unconvinced, switch to olive oil.

The *salade croquante,* or "crisp salad," refers to one made from hearts of romaine, torn and dressed with a simple vinaigrette: 2 tablespoons red wine vinegar to 5 tablespoons extra virgin olive oil, sea salt, and freshly ground pepper.

When I cooked with Alain in New York, he used different kinds of peppercorns, and his steak au poivre was the best I have ever tasted. I've pared it down to two.

Pepper-Crusted Rib Steak

1/4 cup	black peppercorns
1/4 cup	Szechuan peppercorns
2-pound	rib steak on the bone, trimmed of excess fat, trimmings reserved
1/4 cup	olive oil
2 tablespoons plus 2 teaspoons	unsalted butter
	fine sea salt
6 cloves	garlic, unpeeled
2	shallots, finely chopped
1/4 cup	Cognac
2 cups	Beef Jus (page 200)
1/4 cup	heavy cream
1 1/2 teaspoons	Dijon mustard

Put the peppercorns on a baking sheet and crush them with the back of a saucepan. Sieve and reserve both the coarse pieces and the dust separately. Rub the steak with 2 tablespoons of the olive oil, then dredge on both sides in the coarse pieces of pepper. Press the pepper into the beef.

Heat 1 tablespoon of the butter and the remaining 2 tablespoons oil in a large cast-iron skillet over medium heat. Salt the beef and put the steak in the pan; scatter the cloves of garlic around it. Brown the steak on each side for 2 minutes. Add another 1 tablespoon butter and the reserved beef trimmings and reduce the heat to medium. Cook, basting the steak often with the pan juices, until medium-rare, or 5 to 7 minutes on each side. Transfer the steak to a wire rack set over a plate, cover loosely with foil, and let rest for 10 minutes in a warm place.

Meanwhile, make the sauce: Discard the garlic cloves in the skillet and drain off all but 2 tablespoons fat. Add the shallots and cook over medium heat, stirring frequently, until soft, about 2 minutes. Add the Cognac, scraping up the brown bits from the bottom of the pan; simmer until most of the liquid has evaporated. Add the beef jus and simmer until slightly reduced, about 3 minutes. Stir in the cream and simmer until the sauce is thick enough to coat the back of a spoon, 3 to 5 minutes.

Strain the sauce through a fine sieve and return to the pan over medium-low heat. Gradually whisk in the mustard and 2 teaspoons butter cut into small pieces. Season the sauce and thin, if necessary, with more cream.

Slice the steak and serve with some of the sauce poured over it. Pass the remaining sauce in a hot sauceboat on the side.

"One-Armed" Rib-Eye Steak with Black Bean Sofrito

ROBERT MCGRATH

SERVES 4

2	large yellow onions, sliced in 1/4-inch-thick strips or "julienne"
1 cup	diced raw bacon (about 5 ounces)
1 cup	sliced scallions, cut on the diagonal
1/2 cup	garlic cloves, coarsely chopped
1 cup	cooked black beans
1/2 cup	thinly sliced roasted, peeled, seeded fresh poblano peppers
2	large tomatoes, seeded, coarsely chopped
1/2 cup	chopped cilantro leaves (1 big bunch, stemmed)
4 tablespoons	unsalted butter
	kosher salt and freshly cracked black pepper
4	(18-ounce) bone-in rib-eye steaks, with the bone scraped clean*
2 tablespoons	white truffle oil (optional, but really good)
1 cup	crumbled queso fresco

Robert calls this a "one-armed steak" because when he broke his right (steak-flipping) arm, he decided to leave a 6-inch-long rib bone in each steak to make it easy to flip the steaks with his left hand.

The sofrito would be good with grilled or roast chicken as well; sometimes Robert adds kernels of fresh corn for the last 4 minutes of cooking. While he gets a marvelous smoky flavor by literally smoking his onions, you can cook them until lightly charred on a cast-iron stove-top grill. It works well.

Smoke the onion strips over hickory wood or charcoal in a small smoker or in a covered kettle grill with the cover closed, until the onion is translucent.

Sauté the bacon in a skillet over medium heat for 5 minutes, until the fat begins to render. Add the scallions, garlic, black beans, roasted poblanos, and smoked onions and continue to cook for 5 minutes, stirring frequently. Add the tomatoes and cilantro. Cook for another 5 minutes, then stir in the butter. Season the sofrito with salt and pepper to taste.

Ask your butcher to do this for you, if you like.

Continued

Heat a cast-iron skillet until it is very, very hot. Season the steaks thoroughly, but not excessively, with salt and pepper and blast sear them on the cast iron to the desired degree of doneness. Immediately before removing the steaks from the skillet, drizzle the truffle oil over the meat.

Place each steak on a large heated plate and spoon the sofrito over the top where the bone leaves the meat. Sprinkle the queso over the top of each steak and serve.

CHARLIE TROTTER

SERVES 4

Charlie serves tenderloin steaks with arugula-flavored polenta cakes (page 65), and sliced Savoy cabbage, cooked in salted water for 5 minutes, then sautéed in butter and vinegar for another 5 minutes. Each serving gets 2 tablespoons of yellowfoot mushroom sauce (sautéed in butter and water, pureed, and seasoned). But as Charlie points out in the show, all recipes are moveable feasts, and you can pick your own garnishes to go with the polenta cakes; or use chanterelle mushrooms, or portobellos, and so on. The mushrooms should be in roughly 1-inch pieces.

Beef Tenderloin with Yellowfoot Mushrooms

2 tablespoons	grapeseed oil
4 medallions	beef tenderloin, 3 ounces each
	sea salt and freshly ground pepper
2 cups	yellowfoot mushrooms, sliced
2	shallots, finely chopped
1 recipe	Crisp Arugula-Polenta Cakes (page 65)
1/2 cup	Meat Jus (page 201)
	braised cabbage or vegetable garnish of choice

Heat the oil in a sauté pan over medium-high heat. Season the medallions with salt and pepper and sear on both sides for 30 seconds. Reduce the heat to low and add the mushrooms around the beef. Cook for 3 minutes, or until the mushrooms start to give up their liquid, then add the shallots. Salt the mushrooms lightly.

Meanwhile, heat the polenta cakes by sautéing them gently in butter or oil.

Continue to cook the beef, turning once, for another 5 to 8 minutes, until medium-rare. Put the medallions on a plate to rest and keep them warm with the mushrooms. Pour the fat out of the pan and deglaze with the meat jus.

Charlie Trotter's Beef Tenderloin with Yellowfoot Mushrooms.

To serve, put a hot polenta cake in the center of each of 4 hot plates. Spoon the mushroom sauce around the outer edge of the flat part of the plate. Put the cabbage or whatever vegetable garnish you please on top of the polenta and around the plate. Spoon the mushrooms on top of the vegetable and around the base of the polenta cakes. Slice the meat and arrange on top of the mushrooms. Finally, spoon the meat sauce over the sliced beef and present at once.

Jeremiah and Jean-Marie Lacroix in the kitchen.

JEREMIAH TALKS ABOUT

Jean-Marie Lacroix Lacroix at The Rittenhouse, Philadelphia

JEAN-MARIE WALKS WITH THE ASSURANCE OF A CHEF who has cooked long enough to know exactly what he is doing, yet not so long that the passion has left. He seems to know that not much has to be said before the plates of food arrive, because they say it all.

I was not prepared for what greeted me as I walked out of the elevator doors, turned left, and saw the sign LACROIX. Its perfect, discreet lettering reminded me at once of something new, and of something wonderfully familiar. As it turned out, rarely has such a first visual impression been so on the money to describe what Jean-Marie and his restaurant are all about.

When I entered the restaurant I was immediately enveloped in the heady perfume of what I saw twenty feet in front of me against the windows looking out onto Rittenhouse Square: a ten-foot altar covered with enormous, ripe pomelos sitting on a bed of aromatic limes. My mouth started to water. A brilliant touch—as was the color of the upholstery, a green that must be identical to the color of the leaves on the hundreds of trees on the square for a few days at the very start of spring.

Jean-Marie's food has a sureness of touch. Every fully flavored dish I tasted reminded me how he took the best flavors of the past and combined them in a new way. A small square of goat cheese and chard lasagna, sauced with lamb braised in the *ancien* style, boasted all the depth of flavor of *grande bourgeoise* cooking without any of its physical weight. A newly conceived yet classic sweetbread and truffle crepinette brought me to tears of both remembrance and love for the future. Iced Spinning Creek oysters with champagne vinegar and shallot sauce posed an astonishing contrast, their cold shells stuck into a little mound of imperially rich, hot mashed potatoes. This last dish illustrates most clearly Jean-Marie's unique touch of taking the flavors of the past and presenting them with a modern sense of humor.

Veal Medallions with Caramelized Belgian Endive and Coffee Foam

JEAN-MARIE LACROIX

SERVES 4

1 cup	milk
1 teaspoon	coffee beans, crushed
3	Belgian endives, cut in half lengthwise, cored, then sliced crosswise 1/2 inch thick
2 tablespoons	freshly squeezed lemon juice
1 teaspoon	sugar
	salt and freshly ground white pepper
4 tablespoons	olive oil
2 tablespoons	butter
4	loin of veal medallions, 5 to 6 ounces each
1 cup	dry white wine
2 cups	Veal Stock (page 199)

Put the milk and crushed coffee beans in a small saucepan and heat without letting the milk boil. Remove from the heat and let infuse for 10 minutes. Strain the coffee milk into a small pitcher and refrigerate until chilled.

Put the endives in a bowl and toss them with the lemon juice, sugar, salt, and white pepper. Heat 2 tablespoons of the olive oil with the butter over medium heat in a sauté pan. Add the endives, cover, and cook for 5 minutes. Uncover and finish cooking the endives until the liquid has evaporated and the endives become slightly caramelized, about 5 minutes. Keep warm.

Season the medallions of veal with salt and white pepper. Heat the remaining 2 tablespoons olive oil in a sauté pan. Add the medallions and sear on each side for 2 minutes, until they have a little color. Lower the heat and finish cooking them for 4 to 5 minutes. Remove the medallions and keep warm on a wire rack over a plate.

Pour the fat out of the sauté pan and pour in the white wine. Boil the wine, scraping up any brown bits from the bottom of the pan until it is reduced by two-thirds; then add the veal stock. Boil until the sauce is reduced by half. Add the sauce to the endives, toss them in the sauce, and reheat.

Continued

Cooking in the kitchen of a friend of Jean-Marie, we did not have an espresso machine to make the foam on the milk, so he used an immersion blender. You could also use an immersion blender, or beat the hot, coffee-infused milk like crazy with a whisk.

We used veal from a farm just outside Philadelphia. You should use the whitest veal you can find.

Froth the coffee-flavored milk on the steam jet of an espresso machine (or with a hand mixer or immersion blender) until there is a good head of foam.

To serve, arrange the hot endives with their sauce in the middle of each of 4 hot plates. Set a veal medallion on top of each mound of endive. Spoon a dollop of coffee-milk foam on top of the veal so that it falls over the endive as well.

KEN ORINGER

SERVES 6 TO 10

Ken serves this roast pig with little individual gratins of sweet potatoes, pureed and topped with a layer of grated Beaufort cheese (or Gruyère or Emmenthaler) and finished under the broiler.

He cooks the Belgian endive *sous-vide*, or in a sealed plastic bag, before caramelizing them in butter and sugar, because the bag prevents any oxidization, or discoloration, of the endive and keeps the moisture to a minimum so that the endive needs no wringing out before finishing.

Roast Suckling Pig with Caramelized Belgian Endive

2 cups	canola oil
2 bunches	fresh thyme
1 cup	chopped peeled fresh ginger
1 cup	chopped parsley
1 cup	chopped garlic
1	fresh suckling pig, 20 to 30 pounds
1 recipe	Caramelized Belgian Endive with Orange and Honey (recipe follows)

Mix together the oil, thyme, ginger, parsley, and garlic and rub all over the pig. Keep turning the pig in the marinade and rubbing it over the pig for at least 6 hours or overnight.

Wire the pig to a spit and roast it over a wood or hardwood charcoal fire for 4 to 6 hours, depending on the size of the pig. It will be done when the legs feel tender, move easily in their joint, and any juices, which emerge when a skewer is stuck into the thickest part of the leg, run clear. Then scrape away the fire so that the pig stays only warm. Let the pig rest, still turning, for 30 minutes. Carve and serve with the caramelized endive.

Caramelized Belgian Endive
with Orange and Honey

8	Belgian endives
1/2 cup	sugar
1/2 cup	freshly squeezed orange juice
1/4 cup	honey
6 tablespoons	unsalted butter
	sea salt

Put 2 endives into each of 4 heavy-duty quart-size zipper-seal plastic bags. To each bag, add 1 teaspoon sugar, 2 tablespoons orange juice, 1 tablespoon each honey and butter, and a pinch of salt. Put the bags in a large pot of simmering water and cook until the endives are tender, 20 to 25 minutes. Remove the bags and let cool. Remove the endives from the bag and reserve any cooking juices. Fan out the endives and sprinkle them with the rest of the sugar.

Heat the remaining 2 tablespoons butter over medium heat in a sauté pan big enough to hold all the endives in a single layer until the butter starts to color a light brown. Arrange the endive in the pan in a single layer, sugared side down, and cook very slowly over low heat until they begin to caramelize on the bottom. Do not move them around or rush this cooking process; it will take 8 to 10 minutes. Add the reserved cooking juices or water if the pan juices become too dark or dry up. Cut out the cores at the bottom of the endives and serve them caramelized side up alongside the carved pig.

Ken Oringer's Roast Suckling Pig with Caramelized Belgian Endive, served with a gratin of sweet potatoes.

MARK PEEL

SERVES 6

Spit-Roasted Pomegranate-Marinated Leg of Lamb with Chanterelles

When I saw the outdoor spit barbecue at Mark Peel and Nancy Silverton's house in Los Angeles on a January day that was clear and a balmy 74°, I knew I had to cook outside. After seeing huge fresh chanterelle mushrooms at the Santa Monica Farmer's Market, I then knew we had to cook those under something on the spit, so that the mushrooms would sizzle in the fat and juices dropping onto them from above. We decided upon a leg of lamb.

Marinating the lamb in pomegranate juice acts as a tenderizing agent and provides a flavorful counterpoint to the richness of the lamb.

1	whole leg of lamb, bone in (about 5 to 6 pounds)
1 cup	fresh pomegranate juice
1/4 cup	ruby port
8 cloves	fresh garlic, finely chopped
2 sprigs	fresh rosemary, chopped
2 pounds	fresh chanterelles or other wild mushrooms, brushed clean
4 sprigs	fresh thyme, coarsely chopped
1/4 cup	extra virgin olive oil
	salt and freshly ground pepper
2 cups	chicken stock

Trim any excess fat from the lamb. Mix the pomegranate juice, port, half the garlic, and the rosemary. Rub all over the lamb. Refrigerate the lamb in the marinade, turning it a few times, for 6 hours.

Rub the chanterelles with a mixture of the thyme, remaining garlic, and olive oil. Season with salt and pepper and marinate for 2 hours.

Light a hot fire in a barbecue grill with a rotisserie spit. At the same time, preheat the oven to 350°F.

Remove the lamb from the marinade and pat dry; reserve the marinade. Put the leg on a spit and secure with wire or string. Season the leg with salt and pepper. Put the spit over or, ideally, in front of a hot fire and cook the lamb, while the spit turns, for about 1 1/2 hours, until the meat is medium-rare and the juices still run pink when the leg is pierced in its thickest part with a thin skewer.

When the lamb begins to cook, season the mushrooms with salt and pepper and put them in the oven. Roast for 20 minutes. Transfer them to a shallow baking pan and set in front of the fire under the lamb. Let them continue cooking until tender, turning them twice.

America's Best Chefs Cook *with* Jeremiah Tower

Strain the reserved marinade into a saucepan and add the chicken stock. Bring to a boil, skimming. Continue to boil until the sauce is reduced by half.

When the lamb is cooked, let it rest for 15 minutes away from the fire but still kept warm by it; then take it off the spit. Slice and serve with the sauce poured over the meat and the mushrooms around it.

> *Never wash wild mushrooms, just wipe them [with a damp cloth to get the sand or bits of leaves off them], or they will turn into a big soggy mess. People forget that food comes from the earth.*
>
> —MARK PEEL

(Above) Mark Peel's Spit-Roasted Pomegranate-Marinated Leg of Lamb with Chanterelles. (At left) Chanterelle mushrooms catching the drippings from the lamb.

Nancy Silverton and Mark Peel Campanile, Los Angeles

WHEN I ASKED MARK PEEL WHAT WE WERE GOING TO COOK AT HIS HOUSE in Los Angeles, he said, "Let's go down to the farmers' market and find out." Nancy would do the desserts. In the balmy and sunny air high above the beach in Santa Monica, Mark told me that he had trees full of ripening Meyer lemons and clementine oranges, an outdoor fireplace with a spit, and a temperature-controlled cheese cellar at the restaurant from which I could choose whatever cheeses I wanted. Those four things were to be the basic building blocks of the menu.

The bounty of the farmers' stalls filled in the details: We could not resist the huge, old-rose-colored and juice-filled-to-bursting pomegranates; the heads of radicchio that were pale green and cream-colored with leaves shot with streaks of magenta; anything from the stall piled high with wild mushrooms like the sweet-tooths; the pure white and almost pulsatingly fresh cauliflowers cut that morning, the stalk ends still white and moist; anything from the stall with the most perfect, sulfur-free dried (hardly a word that described the plump fruits lovingly

Mark Peel and Jeremiah at the farmer's market in Santa Monica.

laid out in the sun) fruits and new-crop nuts; the baskets overflowing with freshly picked green and pink heads of garlic; and the enormous bunches of glowing Italian or flat leaf parsley—and certainly not a couple of little boxes of *fraises de bois*.

It was wonderful menu shopping with Mark, since all one of us had to do was mention one word, like cauliflower, and the other would start to fill in the blanks.

"How about a sauce with salted anchovies," I asked.

"Yes, and capers and my Meyer lemons, and that wonderful parsley over there," was Mark's response to complete a dish neither one of us had ever cooked before.

After cooking all day, we went over to his restaurant Campanile and sat outside for a moment to take in the sights of Nancy's La Brea bakery a few feet to the side of the restaurant entrance, of the pink sky turning dark, and of the tastes of our blanc de blancs champagne as we watched the sleek L.A. cars pull up to disgorge the even sleeker Los Angelinos. That night at Campanile the tasting menu made up from the market that morning was:

> Radicchio salad with clementines, Meyer lemon,
> and toasted Serra da Estrella cheese

> Rack of Bruce Campbell Sonoma lamb
> marinated in pomegranate and green garlic

> Roasted sweet-tooth mushrooms and cippolini onions

> Steamed cauliflower with yellowtail roe,
> anchovy and parsley

> Date vanilla bombe with tangerine sherbet
> and walnut meringue

Inside the rustic and comfortable Californian-Mediterranean architecture of Campanile, it was all about those superbly fresh market ingredients, cooked to show them off as elegantly simple as the warm yeasty bread from next door, and a staff who more than forgave me for being dressed in L. L. Bean instead of Gucci. But, then, what can you expect from two chefs like Mark and Nancy who are still more excited and driven by what was in the market that morning than what's in the parking lot?

PHILIPPE BOULOT

Seven-Hour Braised Leg of Lamb

SERVES 6 TO 8

I cannot think of a dish better suited for a large winter dinner party than this one, since it needs to be made a day or two in advance, and once finished, is strictly a reheat. It is a dish that is very difficult to ruin. This is always called seven-hour leg of lamb, but, in truth, it really only takes five.

Philippe serves this lamb with a puree of flageolet beans cooked with bacon, or with assorted vegetables. He garnishes the whole dish with chopped Italian parsley.

1	large leg of lamb, bone in (6 to 8 pounds)
1/4 cup	finely chopped garlic plus 1/2 cup peeled whole garlic cloves
1/2 cup	olive oil
	salt and freshly ground pepper
2	red onions, coarsely chopped
2	carrots, coarsely chopped
6 stalks	celery, coarsely chopped
2 sprigs	fresh rosemary
4 sprigs	fresh thyme
1 tablespoon	coriander seeds, toasted
1 tablespoon	juniper berries
6	bay leaves
2 tablespoons	tomato paste
1/4 cup	all-purpose flour
1 bottle	rich red wine, such as Syrah or Côtes du Rhone

Rub the leg of lamb all over with the chopped garlic, half the olive oil, and salt and pepper. Marinate in the refrigerator 12 hours or overnight.

Preheat the oven to 450°F.

Wipe the garlic off the lamb and brown the leg in the oven in a roasting pan for 20 minutes.

Heat the remaining 1/4 cup olive oil in a flameproof casserole or heavy roasting pan large enough to hold the leg. Add the red onions, carrots, celery, whole garlic cloves, rosemary, thyme, coriander seeds, juniper berries, and bay leaves. Cook the vegetables over high heat, stirring occasionally, until browned, about 10 minutes; do not let them burn. Reduce the heat and add the tomato paste and flour. Mix well into the vegetables. Pour in the red wine, stirring up any brown bits from the bottom of the pan. Add 8 cups water. Cook over medium heat, stirring, for 2 minutes to make sure all the flour is dissolved. Bring to a boil.

Reduce the oven temperature to 275°F.

Philippe Boulot's Seven-Hour Braised Leg of Lamb, served with broccoli, carrots, and Brussels sprouts: (above) the finished dish; (below) a work in progress.

Place the lamb in the casserole, cover with foil and then the lid of the casserole, and cook in the oven for 5 hours, or until the lamb is spoon tender.

Take the lamb out of the liquid and cover with a damp towel. Strain the cooking juices into a saucepan; simmer, while skimming off all fat and scum. Boil to reduce slightly and serve poured over the carved lamb.

Broccoli Rabe and Melted Garlic-Stuffed Lamb Chops

SERVES 6

Nancy serves these chops
with the Potato "Risotto"
(page 141) and the Roasted
Mushrooms (page 139).

2 bunches	broccoli rabe
1/4 cup	peeled whole garlic cloves
1/3 cup plus 2 tablespoons	olive oil
1/2 cup	panko bread crumbs*
1/2 cup	Italian parsley leaves
1/2 cup	mascarpone or cream cheese
1 teaspoon	freshly grated lemon zest
	kosher salt and freshly ground pepper
6	"porterhouse" lamb chops, cut 2 inches thick

Strip the leaves and flowers from the stems of the broccoli rabe and set aside. Parboil the stems in salted boiling water until tender, drain, and immerse them in a bowl of ice water. Drain the stems again, squeeze tightly to remove all the water, and then coarsely chop them.

Put the garlic in a small microwave container and pour in 1/3 cup of the olive oil. Microwave on high for 2 minutes, or until the garlic cloves are soft when pierced with the tip of a small knife. Remove the container and strain the garlic, reserving the garlic-flavored oil for another use (like pasta with clams).

Put the panko and parsley leaves in a food processor and pulse until the bread crumbs turn green; scrape into a medium bowl. Put the reserved broccoli rabe leaves and flowers in the food processor with the chopped stems; puree. Add the mascarpone (or cream cheese) and pulse several times, until just combined. Add this mixture, the lemon zest, and the cooked garlic to the bread crumbs and mix well, mashing the garlic to a paste. Season with salt and pepper to taste.

Preheat the oven to 375°F.

Cut the meat with a boning knife from both sides of the T-bone, but leave the meat attached at the top of the "T." Season both sides of

Panko are coarse, crisp Japanese bread crumbs that can be found in Asian grocery stores and specialty food markets.

the meat. Press about 1/4 cup of the breadcrumb stuffing firmly onto each side of the bone and then replace the meat. Wrap and tie string around the perimeter of the chop, going around twice. Season the meat again with salt and pepper.

Heat a large ovenproof sauté pan over high heat. Add the remaining 2 tablespoons oil, heat for a few seconds, and then add the chops. Turn the lamb chops with tongs to brown them on all sides, beginning with the fatty edges. Remove the chops and discard the fat in the pan. Return the chops to the pan and stand them on the T-bone (so that the meat is not touching the surface of the pan). Cook for 15 minutes, or until the meat registers 130°F (medium-rare) on an instant-read thermometer. Remove from the oven, cover, and keep warm for 15 minutes before serving.

It's no secret that I am a meat lover, but no matter how perfectly cooked, how good the quality, or what it's served with, just seeing a big ol' grilled chop sitting in the middle of a plate gets boring. So you'll often find our [Boulevard Restaurant, San Francisco] meat dishes rolled, wrapped, or stuffed in unusual ways. These lamb chops are a good example.

Here we've taken an extra-thick lamb porterhouse or "T-bone," cut the meat away from the length of the bone, but left it attached at the "T." Then we press a stuffing made from peppery broccoli rabe up against the bone, put the meat back, and tie the whole thing up again, so it looks like an ordinary chop but with a delicious surprise. It's a deceptively simple way to make something rather ordinary special. Try it for your next dinner party and bask in the oohs and aahs as your guests cut into the meat and find that stuffing.

—NANCY OAKES

Nancy Oakes's Broccoli Rabe and Melted Garlic-Stuffed Lamb Chop.

SERVES 6

Pistachio-Crusted Grilled Rack of Lamb with a Carrot-Ginger Essence

Both the mustard-brown sugar glaze and the carrot-ginger essence can be made 2 days ahead of time and held, covered, in the refrigerator. Patrick serves these chops with toasted whole shelled pistachios and Brussels sprout leaves cooked 5 minutes in boiling salted water, buttered, and seasoned.

3 racks	lamb, about 1 1/2 pounds each, bones scraped clean, or "Frenched"
	salt and freshly ground pepper
4 cups	organic carrot juice
2 tablespoons	crème fraîche or sour cream
1 1/2 teaspoons	finely chopped peeled fresh ginger
1 cup	brown sugar
1 cup	Dijon mustard
2 cups	pistachio nuts, shelled, lightly toasted

Preheat the oven to 400°F. Fire up the broiler or grill.

Season the racks of lamb with salt and pepper and grill or broil, turning, until crisp and slightly charred on the outside, 5 minutes on each side. Remove from the grill and set aside.

Put the carrot juice in a medium saucepan and cook over medium heat until reduced by half. Remove from the heat. Whisk in the crème fraîche. Add the ginger and a pinch of salt. Allow the ginger to steep for 10 minutes and then strain. Set the carrot sauce aside.

Combine the brown sugar and mustard in a bowl; blend well. Brush the racks with this mustard–brown sugar glaze and put them in a roasting pan, fat side up. Roast for 10 to 12 minutes.

Meanwhile, finely chop enough of the pistachios to yield 1 1/2 cups. Remove the lamb from the oven and when just cool enough to handle, dip the fat side of the racks into the chopped pistachios. Return to the oven for another 3 to 4 minutes. Remove the racks from the oven and let rest for 3 minutes.

Reheat the carrot sauce. Slice the racks into individual chops. Place them in the center of each of 6 heated plates and splash the carrot sauce around the lamb. Garnish with the remaining whole toasted pistachio nuts.

Patrick O'Connell's Pistachio-Crusted Rack of Lamb with a Carrot-Ginger Essence.

Rack of Lamb
with Crisp Polenta

2 racks	lamb, about 2 pounds each, trimmed
5 tablespoons	extra virgin olive oil
3 tablespoons	chopped mixed fresh herbs, such as rosemary, thyme, marjoram
3/4 cup	Meat Jus (page 201)
	salt and freshly ground pepper
1 recipe	Crisp Polenta (page 65)

Rub the racks of lamb with 3 tablespoons of the olive oil and 2 tablespoons of the herbs. Refrigerate and marinate overnight.

Preheat the oven to 450°F.

Heat a large ovenproof pan over medium-high heat, add the remaining 2 tablespoons olive oil, and sear the lamb on all sides. Transfer to the oven and roast for 8 to 12 minutes, or until slightly less than the desired degree of doneness. Remove the pan from the oven and allow the lamb to rest for 5 minutes.

Meanwhile, put the remaining 1 tablespoon herbs in a small piece of cheesecloth and tie with kitchen string to form a sachet. Put the reduced meat juices in a small saucepan and bring to a simmer over medium heat. Then put the sachet in the sauce and simmer for 3 minutes.

Slice each rack between the bones just prior to serving. Season with salt and pepper to taste. Remove the sachet from the juices and pour the sauce over and around the chops. Serve with the hot, golden, and crisp polenta.

CHARLIE TROTTER

SERVES 4

Only Charlie could discover the magic flavor combination of corn and lamb.

Meats

L'Etoile's Spinach-and-Mint Stuffed Lamb

SERVES 4

Odessa Piper developed this recipe for the legs of lamb from Janie Crawford's farm. Since the recipe calls for only 4 to 6 ounces of lamb per person, this is a very economical dish. Odessa bones the leg and takes out each separate muscle, removes the 'white' skin and tendons, and then pounds out the meat to form a steak a little more than 1/4 inch thick before rolling it up around the spinach and mint stuffing.

She uses feta cheese from Capriole in Blue River, Wisconsin, but any fresh, white, tender, nonsalty feta-style goat cheese will do. You will need a large (gallon-size) freezer-strength plastic bag and a mallet for pounding out the lamb.

4 pieces	boneless leg of lamb, 4 to 6 ounces each, trimmed of all fat and membrane
6 tablespoons	olive oil
1 bag (10 ounces)	young spinach, stemmed, washed, drained
	salt and freshly ground pepper
1/2 cup	fresh mint leaves
1/2 cup	crumbled fresh feta cheese
1	onion, finely chopped
1/2 cup	flat leaf parsley, chopped
2 cups	lamb or chicken stock
1 cup	couscous
1/2 cup	dried red currants

Working with one piece at a time, put the pieces of lamb in a plastic bag with all but one of the edges cut off and gently pound the lamb until it forms a cutlet 1/4 inch thick and about 6 inches by 4 inches.

Heat 2 tablespoons of the olive oil in a large sauté pan over medium heat until a drop of water splashed into it splatters. Then add the spinach, season with salt and pepper, and toss for 1 minute. Add the

Odessa Piper's Spinach-and-Mint Stuffed Lamb from L'Etoile

mint leaves and toss again. Cook until the spinach is half wilted, about 3 minutes. Remove from the pan and let cool.

Arrange the spinach mixture equally along one edge of each flattened lamb piece and sprinkle the feta on top. Roll up the lamb tightly, folding in the ends before the last turn. Make sure you roll in the appropriate direction so that when the cooked lamb is sliced, the cut is against the grain.

Preheat the oven to 400°F.

Heat 2 or 3 tablespoons of the olive oil in a medium sauté pan over medium heat. Season the lamb rolls with salt and pepper and sear them in the pan, turning until nicely browned all over, about 5 minutes. Transfer to the oven and roast for 10 minutes.

Meanwhile, put the onion and remaining olive oil in the sauté pan, cover, and cook over low heat until the onion is softened and translucent, about 5 minutes. Add the parsley and cook uncovered for 1 minute. Pour in the stock. Bring to a boil and add the couscous and 1/2 teaspoon salt. Return to a boil and mix in the currants. Cover and cook over very low heat, adding more liquid if necessary, until the couscous is tender and has absorbed the liquid, about 20 minutes.

Serve with a bed of the couscous in the center of each of 4 hot large plates. Cut each roll diagonally across the grain into 3 or 4 sections and place in a pile against each other in the center of the couscous.

Pan-Fried Sweetbreads with Barigoule of Spring Vegetables

3	large Braised Sweetbreads (recipe follows), cut in 3-ounce medallions
1/2 cup	clarified butter, melted
1 cup	fresh white bread crumbs
	salt and freshly ground pepper
1 recipe	Barigoule of Spring Vegetables (page 135)

Soak the sweetbread medallions in half of the melted butter for 1 minute. Put the bread crumbs in a shallow dish.

Continued

PHILIPPE BOULOT

SERVES 4 TO 6
AS AN APPETIZER

Most everyone these days cooks sweetbreads for a finished dish from the raw state, a practice that short-changes the potential flavor and texture of the sweet-breads, giving them a bad reputation. But if you braise them first on a flavorful bed of "aromatics" (Aromatic Vegetable Mix, page 207) and fresh herbs, the sweetbreads take on a more complex flavor as well as a smooth and unctuous texture.

JEREMIAH TOWER

SERVES 4

Any sweetbread preparation must begin with soaking and braising, and the sweetbreads taste even more wonderful if they are cooked a day before serving.

Transfer the sweetbreads to a plate and season on both sides with salt and pepper. Press the medallions into the bread crumbs until well coated on both sides.

Heat the remaining melted butter in a large heavy frying pan over medium heat. Cook the medallions on each side until golden—about 3 minutes—and serve with the barigoule of vegetables.

Braised Sweetbreads

4	large whole fresh sweetbreads
2	lemons, cut in half
2 cups	finely diced Aromatic Vegetable Mix (page 207)
2	bay leaves
2 sprigs	fresh thyme
4 sprigs	fresh parsley
2 cups	chicken, veal, or beef stock (pages 192, 199, 200)
1/2 cup	dry white wine

Soak the sweetbreads in salty, cold water for 2 hours, changing the water whenever it becomes bloody. Drain the sweetbreads and put them in a pot. Add cold water to cover by 2 inches, squeeze the lemon juice into the water, and then add the lemons. Bring to a boil, remove from the heat, and let stand for 15 minutes. Drain, put the sweetbreads in a colander, cover with ice, and run cold water over them for 5 minutes.

Reheat the oven to 375°F.

Put the vegetable mix, bay leaves, and thyme and parsley sprigs in a casserole just large enough to hold the sweetbreads in a single layer. Cover and cook in the oven for 15 minutes.

Put the sweetbreads on the vegetable mix, pour the stock and wine over them, and season lightly. Reduce the oven temperature to 325°F and braise in the oven, covered, for 45 minutes. Remove the casserole from the oven.

Lift out the sweetbreads, brush off any vegetable mix clinging to them, put them in a bowl, and strain the cooking liquid over them. Let the sweetbreads cool in the liquid.

Roasted Venison Tenderloin with Huckleberry "Grand Veneur" Sauce

PHILIPPE BOULOT

SERVES 4 TO 6

2 pounds	boned venison tenderloins, 2 to 3 inches in diameter, trimmed of silver membrane
	freshly ground pepper
1 pound	thinly sliced applewood-smoked bacon
4	large shallots, finely chopped
4 tablespoons	butter
1/4 cup	huckleberry or lingonberry jam
1 1/2 cups	pinot noir
1/2 cup	Meat Jus (page 201)
1/4 cup	fresh or frozen huckleberries or blueberries
	salt
	deep-fried sage leaves, for garnish

Philippe serves the venison with the Bourbon Acorn Squash on page 148 and deep-fried sage leaves. He also offers a garnish of grilled mushrooms and sautéed squash blossoms.

Preheat the oven to 450°F.

Season the tenderloins with a little black pepper and wrap them in the slices of bacon, so that the slices overlap and cover all the loin but

Continued

Philippe Boulot's Roasted Venison Tenderloin.

the ends of the tips. If the ends are very thin, fold them under. Put the wrapped venison tenderloins on a rack without crowding in a shallow baking pan and set in the oven. Reduce the heat to 350°F and roast to medium-rare, about 45 minutes. Remove from the oven and let rest in a warm place.

Meanwhile, in a medium frying pan, cook the shallots in the butter over low heat, covered, until soft and translucent, about 5 minutes. Add the jam and cook uncovered for another 5 minutes, until slightly caramelized. Pour in the pinot noir and bring to a boil. Add the meat juices and skim off any fat. Boil until the sauce is reduced by half. Add the huckleberries and remove from the heat. Season with salt and pepper to taste.

Slice the venison into medallions 1 1/2 to 2 inches thick. Spoon the sauce over the meat and garnish with deep-fried sage leaves.

America's Best Chefs Cook *with* Jeremiah Tower

Vegetables

ALAIN DUCASSE

SERVES 4

Roast Asparagus with Beef Marrow and Savory Olive Sauce

A very simple dish with huge and pleasurable impact—mostly because of the combination of the marrow and the asparagus.

4	marrow bones
20	thick asparagus spears
1 tablespoon	butter
2 tablespoons	olive oil
1/2 cup	freshly grated Parmesan cheese
1 recipe	Beef Jus (page 200)
48	Niçoise olives, pitted
	sea salt and freshly ground black pepper
1 teaspoon	coarsely ground white pepper

Remove the marrow from the bones, place it in a bowl of cold water with ice cubes, and refrigerate for 6 hours. Drain and cut each piece crosswise in half.

Peel the asparagus and trim the spears so that they are 5 inches long. Rinse in cold water, drain, and dry on a kitchen towel.

In a large skillet, melt the butter in the olive oil over low heat. Place the asparagus in the hot fat and roll them around to coat. Cook, continuing to roll the spears over and over, until they are evenly colored and tender but al dente, about 15 minutes. Sprinkle with the Parmesan cheese and remove from the skillet. Keep warm.

Heat the beef jus, add the olives, cover, and infuse over very low heat without letting the sauce boil.

While the beef jus cooks, bring 2 cups of salted water to a boil in a small saucepan. Plunge the pieces of marrow into the water, reduce the heat to below a simmer, and poach the marrow for 5 minutes.

To serve, ladle a spoonful of the sauce in the center of each of 4 hot plates. Arrange 3 spears of asparagus in the center of each plate, then arrange 2 spears on top of those, crossing at a 90-degree angle. Drain the marrow and arrange 2 pieces on each of the piles of asparagus. Season the sauce with black pepper and surround the asparagus with more sauce, spooning the olives over the asparagus and onto the plate. Sprinkle each piece of marrow with sea salt and white pepper.

America's Best Chefs Cook *with* Jeremiah Tower

Barigoule of Spring Vegetables

PHILIPPE BOULOT

SERVES 4

1 tablespoon	coriander seeds
1/2 cup	extra virgin olive oil
	cayenne
1/4 cup	freshly squeezed lemon juice
1	leek (white and tender green), sliced
12	pearl onions, peeled
16 cloves	garlic, peeled
	sea salt
12	baby carrots, trimmed (leaving 1/8 inch green stem), peeled
12	small radishes, trimmed (leaving 1/8 inch green stem)
4	thick asparagus, peeled, quartered lengthwise
1/2 cup	fresh basil leaves, shredded finely in a "chiffonade"
	freshly ground black pepper

Philippe serves this vegetable ragout with deep-fried sweetbreads, but it is also a wonderful dish served at room temperature by itself as a first course.

Put the coriander seeds and the olive oil in a large nonreactive sauce pan and bring almost to a boil. Remove from the heat and let sit for 15 minutes to infuse the oil.

Add a pinch of cayenne, the lemon juice, leek, pearl onions, garlic, and a pinch of salt to the olive oil. Simmer for 5 minutes. Add the carrots and continue cooking until the onions are barely tender, 5 to 7 minutes. Add the radishes and asparagus and cook for another 3 to 5 minutes, until tender but still firm to the bite.

As soon as the vegetables are cooked, transfer them to a cold metal bowl, cover, and refrigerate until cool. Add the basil and season with salt and pepper. Let marinate 15 minutes and serve at room temperature.

Black Turtle Beans

SERVES 4 TO 6

1 pound	dried black turtle beans
1	onion, chopped
1	carrot, chopped
1 stalk	celery, chopped
1 head	garlic, cut in half
1	Herb Bundle (page 210)
1	ham bone or 1 cup ham scraps
3 quarts	chicken stock
1 tablespoon	ground cumin
1 tablespoon	ancho chile powder
1 tablespoon	salt

Rinse and sort the beans, discarding any stones or discolored beans. Cover the beans with at least 2 inches of cold water and soak overnight; drain. Put the beans in a large pot with fresh cold water to cover by at least 2 inches and bring to a boil. Remove from the heat, let sit for 10 minutes, then drain. Rinse the beans under cold running water.

Wrap the onion, carrot, celery, and garlic in cheesecloth and put in a pot large enough to hold twice the volume of the beans. Add the herb bundle and ham bone. Add the beans. Add the chicken stock and enough cold water to cover the beans and bring to a boil. Skim off any scum that rises to the surface, reduce the heat to low, and simmer until the beans are tender, about 2 hours.

Add the cumin, ancho chile powder, and salt; mix them into the beans. Continue to cook, stirring the beans every 15 minutes to ensure even cooking and to prevent burning on the bottom of the pot. Add more water if the liquid does not cover the beans.

When the beans are cooked, drain them, reserving the liquid for soup or for finishing the beans in a recipe as for baked black beans.

Steamed Cauliflower with Bottarga Sauce

1	very fresh whole young cauliflower
1/3 cup	extra virgin olive oil
2 tablespoons	finely chopped fresh garlic
4	salted anchovies, rinsed and filleted (page 96), chopped
1/4 cup	capers, rinsed, chopped
2 tablespoons	chopped fresh flat-leaf parsley
2 ounces	tuna roe, or *bottarga*, chopped
1	Meyer lemon, zested and juiced
	sea salt and freshly ground black pepper

Put the cauliflower in a steamer, cover, and cook over simmering water until tender at the core, 15 to 20 minutes.

When the cauliflower is nearly cooked, heat half the olive oil in a small saucepan over low heat and add the garlic. Cook for 3 minutes, or until the garlic softens. Do not let it brown. Then add the anchovies, capers, parsley, and tuna roe. Add 2 tablespoons of the cauliflower steaming water and cook for 1 minute. Remove from the heat and add the juice of the lemon, the remaining olive oil, and a good deal of pepper.

Take the cauliflower out of the steamer and slice it crosswise into 2-inch-thick pieces. Put the slices on a platter with the core ends facing the center. Pour the sauce over the cauliflower and sprinkle with the lemon zest, sea salt, and more pepper.

MARK PEEL

SERVES 4 TO 6

This dish is very South of France, which is how Mark and I felt walking around the Santa Monica Farmer's Market one January afternoon, wondering what to cook. We could hear the crash of the waves along the huge, white, sandy beach, and we thought of Hyeres near Toulon and of lunches with Richard Olney at his house nearby when the air was just as balmy.

We used a steamer, but if you cover the cauliflower, a couscous maker or even just a colander over a pot of simmering water will do.

Mark Peel's Steamed Cauliflower with Bottarga Sauce.

Roast Eggplant and Garlic Terrine

As Charlie pointed out on the show, this is a perfect dish for a party, since it has to be made 6 to 8 hours before it is served so that the combined flavors meld and the texture has time to set as it should. The best terrine to use is a chemically nonreactive one, with sides that are secured with a pin and come away for unmolding.

This is a particularly light, Mediterranean-style terrine, with no eggs, cream, or butter.

3 heads	garlic
2 1/4 cups	extra virgin olive oil
2	large eggplants, peeled, sliced lengthwise 1/2 inch thick
	salt and freshly ground pepper
1 cup	flat-leaf parsley leaves, coarsely chopped
1/2 cup	Maytag blue cheese
1/4 cup	heavy cream
1 cup	mascarpone cheese
1 tablespoon	freshly squeezed lemon juice
2 tablespoons	walnut or hazelnut oil
1/2 cup	arugula leaves, washed, spin-dried
1/2 cup	micro or young mixed greens, washed, spin-dried
1/4 cup	fresh pine nuts, toasted
1 tablespoon	aged balsamic vinegar
	fleur de sel

Preheat the oven to 350°F.

Separate the garlic cloves, peel them, and cook in a small saucepan in 2 cups of the olive oil over as low heat as possible for 1 hour. Remove the garlic from the oil and let cool; reserve the oil for another use.

Meanwhile, arrange the slices of eggplant on a baking sheet in a single layer; brush with olive oil on both sides. Season with salt and pepper. Bake for 30 minutes. Remove from the oven and let cool.

Chop the slow-cooked garlic and mix with the parsley. Season lightly with salt and pepper.

Mix the blue cheese, cream, and mascarpone until smooth. Cover and refrigerate the blue cheese sauce until serving time.

Line a terrine with plastic wrap. Layer slices of baked eggplant on the bottom. Sprinkle some of the garlic-parsley mixture over the eggplant and continue layering, finishing with a layer of eggplant on top. Fold over the plastic wrap and refrigerate for 6 to 8 hours.

Unmold the terrine, remove the plastic wrap, and cut the terrine into 2-inch-thick slices. Put a slice or two on each of 6 room-temperature plates.

Put the lemon juice in a small bowl, add salt and pepper, and whisk in the nut oil.

To serve, spoon a ring of blue cheese sauce around the terrine slices. Dress the greens with the nut oil sauce and scatter around the plate. Garnish with the pine nuts. Drizzle balsamic vinegar and some more extra virgin olive oil over the plate and sprinkle the terrine with fleur de sel and some pepper.

Roasted Mushrooms

1 pound	mixed fresh wild mushrooms (porcini, morel, chanterelles, lobster, etc.)
1 tablespoon	olive oil
1 tablespoon	chopped fresh thyme leaves
	kosher salt and freshly ground pepper

Preheat the oven to 350°F.

Clean the mushrooms with a soft brush or cloth. Put them in a large bowl and toss with the olive oil, thyme, salt, and pepper. Put the mushrooms on a baking sheet and bake for 8 to 10 minutes, or until just tender. Set aside at room temperature for up to 6 hours before serving.

NANCY OAKES

SERVES 4

Like the mushrooms Mark Peel and I cooked under the spit-roasted leg of lamb (page 118), these taste all the more fantastic for cooking under lamb chops, if that is what you are serving them with. But they are also wonderful without the meat juices and, in this version, are purely vegetarian.

ALAIN DUCASSE

SERVES 4 TO 6

Ducasse serves these with
the Pepper-Crusted Rib
Steak on page 110, but they
are so good, I would offer
them with almost any grilled,
baked, or roasted meat, or
as a course by themselves
with the salad mentioned in
the recipe for the steak.

Fried Potatoes

4 pounds	large all-purpose potatoes
2 to 3 cups	water-rendered goose or duck fat (page 209) or olive oil
6 tablespoons	unsalted butter
1 bunch	flat-leaf parsley, stemmed, leaves coarsely chopped
	coarse sea salt

Peel the potatoes and trim each one into a neat rectangle about 3 inches long. Cut each potato lengthwise into 1/2-inch-thick slices, then cut each slice into 1/2-inch strips.

Melt 2 to 3 inches of fat in a large, deep, heavy skillet over medium heat until very hot, 375°F on a deep-frying thermometer.

Thoroughly pat the potatoes dry. Fry them in batches, turning the strips occasionally, until golden brown, 5 to 10 minutes. Drain on paper towels and sprinkle with salt.

When all the potatoes are cooked, pour off the fat and wipe out the skillet. Melt the butter in the same pan. Add the potatoes and heat through, tossing frequently. Add the parsley, season with coarse salt, and serve.

NANCY OAKES

SERVES 6

Chunky Mashed Potatoes with Mascarpone and Arugula

2 pounds	Yukon Gold potatoes (medium to large), peeled, quartered lengthwise
12 cloves	garlic, peeled
8 tablespoons	unsalted butter (1 stick)
1/2 cup	mascarpone cheese
	kosher salt and freshly ground pepper
4 cups	chopped arugula leaves
2 tablespoons	extra virgin olive oil
1 teaspoon	crushed hot red pepper

Put the potatoes in a large saucepan with salted water to cover by 1 inch. Bring to a boil over high heat. Add the garlic and reduce the heat to a simmer. Cook for 15 minutes, or until the potatoes are just tender when pierced with a knife but not falling apart; drain.

Put the potatoes and garlic in a medium bowl with the butter and mascarpone. Mix well with a large spoon or fork, mashing but making sure to leave some of the potatoes in large chunks. (Up to this point the potatoes can be made up to 6 hours in advance.)

Reheat the potatoes in a microwave or over medium-low heat, stirring often. Season with additional salt and pepper to taste.

Sauté the arugula in a large skillet with the olive oil and hot pepper over medium heat until just wilted, 1 to 2 minutes. Fold the arugula into the hot potatoes so that it looks like green marbled streaks.

Potato "Risotto"

NANCY OAKES

SERVES 4

1 pound	Yukon Gold potatoes
2 cups	heavy cream
2 tablespoons	unsalted butter
1 cup	finely diced bacon
1	medium onion, finely chopped
	coarse salt and freshly ground white pepper

Cut the potatoes with a sharp chef's knife or vegetable cutter into even, 1/8-inch-thick slices. Stack the slices and cut them into 1/8-inch-thick strips; then cut crosswise into 1/8-inch cubes. As you cut the potatoes, immerse them in a bowl with the heavy cream. When all the potatoes are cubed, cover the bowl and set aside at room temperature for at least 2 hours, or refrigerate overnight.

Melt the butter in a large saucepan over medium heat. Add the bacon and onion and cook until soft and translucent, about 5 minutes. Strain the potatoes through a fine-mesh sieve, reserving the cream. Put the drained potatoes in the saucepan with the onion and pour in enough cream to just cover and separate the potatoes. Heat the cream until it bubbles around the edges, then reduce the heat to very low.

Continued

Slowly simmer the potatoes in the cream, stirring frequently, until they yield to the bite but still keep their shape, about 10 minutes. Season with salt and white pepper to taste. Serve immediately or set aside at room temperature for up to 2 hours and reheat before serving, either over low heat on top of the stove or in a microwave.

FRANK STITT

SERVES 4 TO 6
AS GARNISH

Frank serves this hearty vegetable mélange with braised guinea hen or sautéed or roast chicken. For a vegetable dish served on its own, double the quantities.

Braised Root Vegetables

2	turnips, peeled, cut in 6 wedges each
1/2	rutabaga, peeled, cut into 1/4- by 2-inch pieces
2	carrots, peeled, cut into 1 1/2-inch pieces
2	cipollini onions, peeled
4 tablespoons	butter
	salt and freshly ground white pepper
1 tablespoon	sugar

Cook the vegetables over low heat in separate covered pans, each with 1 tablespoon butter, 2 tablespoons water, a pinch each salt and white pepper, and 1/4 of the sugar, for 10 minutes. Remove the cover and cook for another 5 minutes, or until tender and glazed.

Oven-Roasted Root Vegetables

JEREMIAH TOWER

SERVES 4 TO 6

2	celery roots, peeled, cut in 6 wedges each
2	parsnips, peeled, any core removed
16	small carrots, peeled, tops removed
2	large Walla Walla Sweets or Vidalia or Maui onions, peeled, quartered
4 sprigs	fresh thyme
1/2 cup	extra virgin olive oil
	salt and freshly ground pepper

Preheat the oven to 325°F.

Put all the vegetables in a bowl. Add the thyme, olive oil, salt, and pepper and toss together. Cover and leave 2 hours, tossing the vegetables together a couple of times to spread the marinade ingredients around evenly.

Put the vegetables in a baking pan, cover, and roast for 1 hour. Remove the cover, turn the vegetables over, and cook for another hour, or until tender. If some finish before others, remove them to the bowl. (If using a covered grill, put the vegetables on a metal baking sheet and put that on the grill.)

Serve plain with lemon juice and extra virgin olive oil or as an accompaniment to other dishes.

Like fruits that improve by concentrating their flavors with a bit of oven drying (see page 204), commercial vegetables can slim down and improve their flavor by losing a bit of their irrigation water. I recommend only root vegetables that are full of starches and sugars (since things like fennel, which I have seen treated this way, just get tough and boring). The exception to the root rule is pumpkin or any of the hard squash like hubbard, acorn, butternut, or turban.

Use celery root, onions, carrots, Jerusalem artichokes, beets, sweet potatoes, potatoes, salsify, rutabagas, parsnip, and turnips. For those with a wild streak, you can also forage and use the root stalks of bullrushes, cattails, spatterdock (water lily), pickerel weed, burdock, groundnut, and day lily.

Using a wood oven produces the most flavorful results, but since almost no one in America has one, I suggest using a covered grill with as little smoke as possible, though a touch makes vegetables taste even better.

Jeremiah cooking with Michael Romano in the kitchen at the Wolfer Estate winery.

Michael Romano Union Square Cafe, New York

"FOOD THAT WILL MAKE YOU HAPPY" is how Michael Romano described his style when we were cooking together at the Wolfer Estate, a winery on Long Island's North Fork. He was referring more specifically to the food at his latest restaurant, Blue Smoke, but it's true about all the food that Michael cooks, and certainly the reason why his flagship restaurant, Union Square Cafe, is consistently voted consistently New York's most popular.

When *The New York Times* called the ribs and potato salad at Blue Smoke the kind of food everyone knows because everyone has a mother and grandmother who's cooked such dishes, I thought it was a true statement of Union Square Cafe as well. That is, when you also add on a brilliant chef and the comfortable décor of a country restaurant with a large bar and wonderful paintings of food on the walls. What the *Times* may or may not have known is that, when cooking or talking about his culinary inspiration, Michael refers constantly to his mother, grandmother, and the amateur-chef aunts who filled his childhood with the techniques and aromas of the food of Naples, Puglia, and Italian New York home cooking.

The first dish he cooked for me was dried spaghetti with *bottarga*, garlic, and perfect Italian olive oil—with bread crumbs baked with olive oil and fresh parsley strewn on top. It was surprisingly light Italian soul food, the saltiness of the roe offset by the sweetness of the oil and parsley. A little of the pasta cooking water incorporated into the sauce made it anything but oily.

Michael served up one dish after another with the grace of a famous chef who still loves to cook, and a man who has never forgotten the women who first put a spoonful of warm sun-ripened tomatoes slowly stewed in smoothly ripe olive oil and basil into his mouth. It did not hurt Michael's popularity with the winery workers that the dessert he served following the superbly fresh codfish, cooked slowly in extra virgin olive oil until it almost had the texture of foie gras, was a chocolate pudding flan and peanut butter cookies.

Sautéed Spinach with Garlic

MICHAEL ROMANO

SERVES 4 TO 6

4 tablespoons	extra virgin olive oil
2 pounds	spinach, stemmed, washed twice, drained (some water left on)
6 cloves	garlic, peeled, slightly crushed
	sea salt and freshly ground pepper

This version of spinach with garlic does not brown the garlic as many Italian recipes do, which results in a lighter, more subtle flavor.

Heat the olive oil in a large frying pan over medium heat. Add the spinach, toss it around for a few seconds, and add the garlic. Season lightly with salt and pepper. Cover the pan and continue to cook for 2 minutes, or until the spinach begins to give up its liquid.

Uncover the pan and cook, stirring constantly, until all the liquid has disappeared, about 2 minutes. Season again and serve.

Baked Tomatoes Confit

ALAIN DUCASSE

MAKES ABOUT 1½ CUPS

4½ pounds	large plum tomatoes, peeled, quartered lengthwise, membranes and seeds removed
6 cloves	garlic, skins on
8 sprigs	fresh thyme
¼ cup	olive oil
2 teaspoons	coarse sea salt

This recipe was taken from Alain Ducasse's *Flavors of France*. In his cookbook, he explains that this preparation of tomatoes is a different choice from sun-dried tomatoes, which are drier and have "... a heavier, more bitter flavor" than this preparation.

Tomatoes confit, used in tarts and salads, and as vegetable side dishes, can be stored for up to 3 days in the refrigerator.

Preheat the oven to the lowest setting and oil a large baking sheet.

Arrange the tomatoes on the baking sheet. Scatter the garlic and thyme over the tomatoes. Drizzle the olive oil over the tomatoes and sprinkle them with the sea salt.

Bake the tomatoes for 2 to 3 hours, turning them over once halfway through the cooking process; the tomatoes will shrink and dry slightly, but they should be quite plump and moist. Remove the tomatoes from the oven and set aside to cool.

Continued

When the tomatoes are cool, put them on a plate with the garlic and thyme, cover with cling film, and refrigerate until needed. If the tomatoes are not going to be used within 24 hours, put them (and the garlic and thyme) in a jar, cover with olive oil, seal the jar, and refrigerate for up to 3 days.

JEREMIAH TOWER

SERVES 4 TO 6

Like the Oven-Dried Pears on page 204, this technique concentrates the flavors and sugars of tomatoes by getting rid of a lot of that irrigation water. They will never be as good as the tomatoes grown outside of Naples in its volcanic soils, when the whole tomato plant, full of ripe tomatoes, is pulled up and hung upside-down on a south-facing wall for a few days—but they are close.

Oven-Cooked Tomatoes

10	ripe tomatoes (red or yellow), cut crosswise in half
1 cup	olive oil
2 taplespoons	chopped garlic
2 tablespoons	fresh rosemary, chopped
2 tablespoons	fresh thyme leaves, chopped
4 tablespoons	kosher salt
2 tablespoons	freshly ground pepper
2 tablespoons	fennel seed, toasted, chopped

Put all the ingredients in a bowl, gently toss, and marinate for 30 minutes.

Preheat the oven to 200°F.

Put a fine-mesh cake rack in a baking sheet and lay the tomatoes out, cut face down, 1/2 inch apart on the rack.

Roast in the oven for 6 to 8 hours or overnight. Remove and let cool. Refrigerate or store in olive oil in the refrigerator.

VARIATION

If you have a smoker, cook the tomatoes in that. Then puree them in fish or chicken stock (or water) and mount them with butter to end up with one of the most haunting sauces ever.

America's Best Chefs Cook *with* Jeremiah Tower

Stuffed Tomatoes

ALAIN DUCASSE

8	ripe red tomatoes, 2 to 3 inches in diameter
	sea salt and freshly ground pepper
1/2 cup	extra virgin olive oil
2 cloves	garlic, unpeeled
1 sprig	fresh rosemary
1 sprig	fresh thyme
2	small white onions, finely chopped
4	Baked Tomatoes Confit (page 145), chopped in 1/4-inch pieces
1 tablespoon	chopped parsley
1 tablespoon	freshly grated Parmesan cheese
1 tablespoon	freshly chopped basil
2 tablespoons	roasted chicken juices or reduced rich chicken stock
2 tablespoons	fresh chives, cut in 1-inch lengths

SERVES 4

Ducasse serves these with the roast chicken on page 98, but they are mind-boggling served just by themselves as a first or vegetable course. Of course, you have to have the "confit" or concentrated tomatoes first (page 145).

When Ducasse serves these with the chicken, he adds a few croutons rubbed with garlic and pan-fried in olive oil, and often adds other vegetables like artichokes cooked whole "barigoule" style (see page 135 for Philippe Boulot's version of barigoule), then stuffed with olive tapenade and braised with the stuffed tomatoes in the oven.

Cut the tops of 4 of the tomatoes about 1/3 the way down from the stem. Save the tops. Scoop out the interiors, salt and pepper the empty cavities, and turn the tomatoes upside down on a baking sheet to drain out excess water. This way you will get a more solid tomato and prevent excess liquid from exuding into the stuffing.

Plunge the remaining tomatoes momentarily into boiling water and then into iced water to loosen the skins. Remove the skins, cut the tomatoes in quarters, and remove the seeds.

Preheat the oven to 375°F.

Heat 2 tablespoons of the olive oil in an ovenproof skillet with the garlic cloves. Add the seeded tomato quarters, the rosemary, and the thyme. Season with salt and pepper to taste. Transfer to the oven and bake until the tomatoes are reduced to a marmalade appearance, about 20 minutes. Remove and let cool.

Remove and discard the garlic cloves, rosemary, and thyme. Mix the chopped onions into the tomato jam. Put in a sauté pan with 2 tablespoons of olive oil and cook, covered, over low heat for 10 minutes.

Continued

Put the tomatoes confit in a bowl with the parsley, Parmesan cheese, basil, and 2 tablespoons of the olive oil. Stir in the tomato-onion jam. Season with salt and pepper.

Reduce the oven temperature to 350°F.

Stuff the drained tomatoes with the tomato marmlade mixture, put the cut tops back on each tomato, drizzle with 2 tablespoons of the olive oil, and place in a gratin dish just large enough to hold them. Bake for 30 minutes. Drizzle regularly with more olive oil and the roasted chicken juices.

Serve the stuffed tomatoes on a plate by themselves or with roasted chicken, and pour the pan juices over them. Add a little freshly ground pepper and sprinkle with the chives.

PHILIPPE BOULOT

SERVES 4

Philippe Boulot's Bourbon Acorn Squash, shown with pom-pom mushrooms.

Bourbon Acorn Squash

2	acorn squash, cut in half lengthwise, peeled, seeds removed
8 tablespoons	unsalted butter (1 stick)
1/2 cup	packed brown sugar
1/2 cup	bourbon
	salt and freshly ground pepper

Cut the squash halves on a vegetable slicer or with a large knife into slices 1/2 inch thick.

Melt the butter in a large sauté pan over medium heat. Add the brown sugar and the bourbon. Bring to a boil and carefully flame off the alcohol. Add the slices of squash, and a pinch of salt; mix well. Reduce the heat to medium-low and cook, stirring occasionally, until the squash is tender but not falling apart, 15 to 20 minutes. Season with salt and pepper to taste and serve.

America's Best Chefs Cook *with* Jeremiah Tower

Warm Mixed Vegetable Stew with Baked Goat Cheese

JEREMIAH TOWER

SERVES 6 TO 8

1	8-ounce fresh, rindless, white goat cheese round
	freshly ground pepper
12 tablespoons	butter (1¹/2 sticks)—4 tablespoons melted, 8 tablespoons cold, cut into pieces
¹/2 cup	fresh white bread crumbs
16	small pearl onions, peeled
1	red bell pepper, cut lengthwise into thin strips
1	yellow bell pepper, cut lengthwise into thin strips
1 sprig	fresh thyme
1 sprig	fresh tarragon
	salt
12	baby red carrots, trimmed, peeled
4	small yellow zucchini, halved lengthwise
12	green French beans
2 pounds	fava bean pods, beans removed and peeled
8	large green asparagus spears, bottom ¹/2 inch of stem cut off, peeled, cut in half across, halved lengthwise
24	fresh squash blossoms (optional)
1 tablespoon	mixed fresh herbs (thyme, marjoram, tarragon, parsley), finely chopped
2 cloves	garlic, finely chopped

The combination here is only one of many, though I never use more than seven to nine vegetables, and I never use tomatoes unless they are cherry tomatoes, because they water down the sauce and dominate the flavors. The addition of chopped garlic and herbs just before you bring the stew to the table causes a burst of rich fragrance that perfects the dish.

I prefer water to chicken stock for a cooking liquid— the resulting sauce has a much fresher and purer vegetable taste—and I use either butter or olive oil to finish

Preheat the oven to 400°F.

Dust the surface of the goat cheese with freshly ground black pepper. Then dip the cheese in the 4 tablespoons melted butter and press it into the bread crumbs to coat all over. Put the cheese in an ovenproof dish and bake in the oven for 10 to 15 minutes, turning once, until golden brown but not melted.

Put the onions, bell peppers, thyme, tarragon, 1 cup of water, and a pinch of salt in a sauté pan. Cover and simmer for 5 minutes.

Meanwhile, bring a large pot of salted water to a boil; maintain it at a steady boil while adding the succession of vegetables. Cook the carrots in the boiling water for 1 minute, then lift them out and add to the

Continued

Jeremiah's Warm Mixed Vegetable Stew.

the dish. If the word ragout comes from the French ragouter, meaning "to revive the appetite," then this is the dish to do it.

In this version, which I cooked with Jean-Marie Lacroix, I served the stew with a Capriole baked fresh goat cheese coated in fresh bread crumbs, and olive oil garlic toasts sprinkled with sea salt.

Jeremiah's Warm Mixed Vegetable Stew with Baked Goat Cheese.

onions in the sauté pan. Cook the zucchini in the boiling water for 1 minute, then add to the other vegetables. Cook the French beans, fava beans, and asparagus together in the boiling water for 1 minute and add to the other vegetables.

Toss, cover, and cook the vegetables for 2 minutes. Make sure there is about 1 cup of liquid in the vegetable pan. Uncover the pan. Add the squash blossoms, herbs, garlic, and remaining 8 tablespoons cold butter. Raise the heat to high and toss the vegetables together until the butter is melted and the sauce thickens a little. Season with salt and pepper to taste and serve immediately on a large platter with the goat cheese in the center.

America's Best Chefs Cook *with* Jeremiah Tower

Desserts

ALAIN DUCASSE

The "Spoon" Chocolate Pizza

MAKES 4 INDIVIDUAL
PIZZAS

I tasted this dessert when I cooked in New York with Alain Ducasse for the television show, and I can tell you that I have never seen a crew hanging over the cameras waiting for the finished dish as they were for this chocolate pizza from Ducasse's "Spoon" restaurants and his cookbook of the same name.

You will need to make the dough the day before and have four 4-inch tartlet forms 1 inch high. The ones with removable bottoms are the easiest.

Brioche crust

2 teaspoons	active dry yeast
2^1/$_2$ tablespoons	warm water
1 cup	all-purpose flour
2 tablespoons	granulated sugar
1 tablespoon	unsweetened cocoa powder
	salt
3	eggs
12 tablespoons	butter for dough (1^1/$_2$ sticks)

Chocolate filling

3 level tablespoons	unsweetened cocoa powder
^{1}/$_4$ cup	brown sugar
3 tablespoons	cold butter, cut in ^{1}/$_4$-inch cubes
^{1}/$_3$ cup	heavy cream
^{1}/$_3$ cup	good-quality bittersweet chocolate, broken in ^{1}/$_4$-inch pieces

Make the brioche crust: Put the yeast and water in a mixing bowl of a countertop mixer and mix until the yeast is dissolved. Add the flour, sugar, cocoa, and a pinch of salt. Mix together on medium speed until the ingredients come together as a dough. Then knead the dough with a bread-hook attachment for 5 minutes, or until the dough pulls away from the edges of the bowl cleanly. Add the eggs and 12 tablespoons butter and mix again until the dough again no longer sticks to the bowl.

Let the dough rise at room temperature for 45 minutes, or until it has doubled in volume. Knead once again briefly until the dough is smooth, shiny, and "dry" to the touch. Place in a bowl dusted with flour, cover with plastic wrap, and refrigerate overnight.

Preheat the oven to 350°F.

Butter four 4-inch tartlet forms 1 inch high. Roll out the dough on a lightly floured board or table until 3/4 inch thick. Cut into 4 circles 8 inches in diameter. Line the forms with the brioche rounds. Prick the dough thoroughly with a fork to avoid air bubbles in the cooked pizza.

For the chocolate filling: Spoon equal amounts of cocoa powder, brown sugar, and butter cubes into each of the brioche shells. Let the shells rise for 20 minutes, so the cooked dough will be a little softer.

Set the shells in the oven on a baking sheet and bake one-third of the way through, or 8 to 10 minutes. Then pour the cream equally over each of the 4 pizzas. Cook for another 8 minutes, until the cocoa, cream, and butter are well mixed and form a liquid.

Turn off the oven, sprinkle the chocolate pieces equally on top of the 4 pizzas, and leave the door ajar for 2 minutes, or until the chocolate melts. Remove the pizzas to a wire rack. When cool enough to handle, remove from the forms and serve the pizzas warm, not hot.

Butterscotch Milkshake

8 tablespoons	butter (1 stick)
2/3 cup	corn syrup
3/4 cup	packed brown sugar
2/3 cup	granulated sugar
1/2 teaspoon	salt
8 scoops	vanilla ice cream
1 cup	half-and-half
1/2 cup	Whipped Cream (page 208)

To make the butterscotch, put 6 tablespoons of the butter and the corn syrup in a heavy saucepan. Cook over medium heat for 5 minutes, stirring occasionally. Then add the brown sugar, granulated sugar, salt, and remaining 2 tablespoons butter. Continue cooking, while whisking, for another 5 minutes. Let cool, then store, covered, in the refrigerator until you need it for the shake—for up to 4 days.

For each shake, put 2 scoops of ice cream and 2 tablespoons each of the prepared butterscotch and the half-and-half in a blender. Puree until smooth. Pour into a cold tall glass and top with whipped cream.

FRANK STITT

MAKES 4 SHAKES

Frank says that this shake started with a surfeit of summer strawberries. When that season ended, they missed the milkshake made from them, so in the winter season, they invented this flavor.

Frank Stitt's Butterscotch Milkshake.

Mini Root Beer Floats

3 cups	very cold root beer
8 tiny scoops	vanilla ice cream

Rest half a drinking straw in each of 8 small serving glasses. Pour in root beer almost to the top. Use the scoop or melon baller to place a round, tiny scoop of ice cream in each cup. Serve immediately.

This is so simple that it barely qualifies as a recipe, but you'd be surprised how people squeal with delight when you bring these floats to the table. I serve them in small, colored metallic cups.

Root beer is a surprisingly good complement to many other dessert flavors, like peanut, vanilla, lemon, butterscotch, and cinnamon. You will need 4 thick drinking straws cut in half, a miniature ice cream scoop or melon baller, and 8 small serving glasses.

—GALE GAND

Pears Poached in Red Wine

4	ripe pears, such as Bosc
1 bottle	young dark red wine
1 cup	port wine
1 cup	sugar
2 pieces	orange peel, each 3 by 1 inch
1 sprig	rosemary
small pinch	salt
1 recipe	Cold Orange Sabayon (recipe follows)

Peel the pears and core them with a melon baller. Cut the pears in half lengthwise and put in a nonreactive saucepan with the wine, port, sugar, orange peel, rosemary, and salt. Simmer for 30 minutes, or until the pears are tender.

With a slotted spoon, transfer the pears to a bowl. Strain the poaching liquid over them. Let stand overnight.

Put the pears aside. Boil the liquid until reduced by half. Pour back over the pears. Let cool again, then serve with the orange sabayon.

Cold Orange Sabayon

6	egg yolks
1/4 cup	orange Muscat wine
3 tablespoons	sugar
1 tablespoon	Grand Marnier liqueur
small pinch	salt

Put all the ingredients in a mixing bowl (or preferably a copper zabaglione bowl) over simmering water, and whisk vigorously until the egg mixture foams, thickens, and forms a firm peak.

Immediately place the bowl into another larger bowl filled with ice and water, and whisk vigorously until cold. Serve at once or store in a covered container in the refrigerator until needed.

SERVES 4

The sabayon must be whisked over ice after it is cooked, or while cooling it will separate. If chilled as instructed here, it will last for up to 3 days in the refrigerator. It can be used as a sauce, or served as a dessert by itself with cookies.

NANCY OAKES

Whole Apple Pecan Crisp

SERVES 6

2 cups	dry white wine
2 cups	apple juice, cider, or French hard cider
1	bay leaf
10	black peppercorns
1	small cinnamon stick
1	cardamom pod
6	medium apples, peeled, cored
1 recipe	Crisp Pecan Topping (recipe follows)
	rum raisin ice cream
1 recipe	Cider Caramel Sauce (page 158)

Nancy speaks for herself with this recipe:

"Most of the desserts on the Boulevard Restaurant menu are the kind I really like to eat. By that I mean that they're the kind of desserts that I would eat at home. Not particularly tempted by elaborate, architectural, or complicated sweet creations, I was inspired by candy apples, the kind you get as a kid at Halloween—whole apples coated with sticky sweet caramel and chopped nuts. What evolved after some experimentation is this very homey but sophisticated dessert that is more like an apple crisp with lots of topping covering the whole poached apple. And instead of coating the apple with caramel, a caramel sauce is served alongside. It's the kind of dessert that will delight the kid in all of us."

The apples: "There are many varieties of apples to choose from, but the quality of the apple will affect the final result. You want an apple that is on the tart side to offset the sweetness of the

Put the wine, apple juice or cider, bay leaf, peppercorns, cinnamon stick, and cardamom in a 3- to 4-quart saucepan. Stir and add the whole apples. Bring the liquid to a simmer and cook until the apples are just barely tender when pierced with a fork, about 20 minutes. Remove the apples with a slotted spoon and set aside to cool.

Strain the poaching liquid into another container, remove 2 cups and put it into a small saucepan. Boil to reduce those 2 cups to $1/2$ cup. Set aside to use in the caramel sauce and then refrigerate the rest of the poaching liquid for another use.

Preheat the oven to 375°F. Butter six 3- by 1-inch ring molds and set them on a nonstick baking sheet. Place a poached apple in each ring mold and then pack the tops equally and tightly with the crisp topping, stuffing some of it into the apple cores and allowing some of it to fall down the sides of the apples and fill up the ring molds. Press on more than you think it will hold, mounding the mixture slightly, because the apples shrink as they cook further.

Bake until the tops are golden and bubbling around the bottom and the apples are warmed through, about 20 minutes. Remove from the oven and set aside to cool slightly before serving.

To serve, run a small knife around the inside edge of the ring molds to release the apples. Slip a spatula under the molds to lift each one into the center of each of 6 plates or shallow bowls. Slip the ring molds off the apples. Top with a scoop of rum raisin ice cream and spoon the cider caramel sauce around.

Crisp Pecan Topping

1 cup	pecans, coarsely chopped
1 cup	all-purpose flour
1 cup	packed brown sugar
8 tablespoons	unsalted butter (1 stick), just barely melted

Preheat the oven to 350°F. Put all the ingredients in a mixing bowl and stir until they form pea-sized clumps, adding more flour if necessary. Spread the mixture on a rimmed baking sheet and bake for 20 minutes, stirring occasionally to break up the mix. Remove from the oven and set aside to cool.

topping and caramel sauce, and one that is able to hold its shape during cooking. The apples we chose after testing, in order of preference, are Fuji, Gala, and Golden Delicious. The apples can be poached a day ahead, and the crisps can be prepared 8 hours before serving and reheated in a 375°F-oven for 10 minutes or until just warmed through."

The molds: "Needed for this recipe are 3- by 1¹/₂-inch straight-sided round ring molds and 2 tablespoons of butter to grease them. You can find these ring molds in better cookware stores. You can also substitute tin cans that, with the tops and bottoms removed, have similar dimensions.

"Serve with rum raisin ice cream, vanilla ice cream, or a whipped cream of your choice."

—NANCY OAKES

Nancy Oakes's Whole Apple Pecan Crisp.

Cider Caramel Sauce

2 cups	apple poaching liquid (page 156)
2 cups	packed brown sugar
8 tablespoons	unsalted butter (1 stick)
4 tablespoons	melted unsalted butter
$1^1/2$ cups	sour cream

Boil the apple poaching liquid until reduced to $^1/2$ cup.

Put the brown sugar and butters in a medium saucepan and cook, while stirring, over medium heat until the brown sugar is dissolved. Increase the heat to high and bring to a boil. Cook for another 2 minutes.

Off the heat, stir in the poaching liquid from the apples. Return to medium heat and cook until the mixture forms a sticky, fudgelike mass. Remove from the heat and whisk in the sour cream. Set aside until serving or refrigerate, covered, for up to 2 weeks.

PATRICK O'CONNELL

Chocolate Bourbon-Pecan Tart

SERVES 6

$1^1/2$ cups	sugar
$^1/3$ cup	water
1 cup	heavy cream
1 cup	pecans
$^1/4$ cup	bourbon
$^1/4$ cup	melted butter
1	egg yolk
1	whole egg
1	pre-baked pie shell (page 208)
4 ounces	bittersweet chocolate, melted

For this rich dessert, you will need a pre-baked 9- or 10-inch tart or pie shell.

Preheat the oven to 350°F.

Put the sugar and water in a heavy 1-quart saucepan and bring to a boil, stirring to dissolve the sugar. Cook over medium heat without stirring until the syrup turns golden brown and then caramel colored. Remove the pan from the heat. Slowly and very carefully pour the cream into the caramel, taking care to protect your face and hands if the cream spatters out of the pan.

Cook the caramel-cream mixture over low heat for 3 minutes, stirring to dissolve any remaining lumps of caramel. Strain the mixture through a fine-mesh sieve and allow to cool for 15 minutes.

Put the pecans on a cookie sheet and toast them in the oven for 5 to 7 minutes, or until lightly browned. Remove and set aside.

Increase the oven temperature to 400°F.

Whisk the bourbon, butter, egg yolk, and whole egg into the cooled caramel mixture. Stir in the toasted pecans.

Brush the pre-baked pie shell with the melted chocolate and pour the pecan filling into the shell. Bake the filled tart in the oven for 15 minutes. Reduce the heat to 350°F and continue baking for an additional 15 minutes.

Serve the tart at room temperature.

> *This chewy confection tastes like the deep South. It keeps beautifully for 3 or 4 days in the refrigerator, and can be cut into very thin wedges to serve with tea, or it can be offered as dessert along with a little bourbon-laced whipped cream. We feature it always on our holiday buffet table during our Christmas open house for the town citizens—a group of bourbon aficionados.*
>
> —PATRICK O'CONNELL

Blackberry-Apple Compote with Lemon

SERVES 4

Jean-Marie fell in love with this kind of simple fruit dessert when living in England with his English wife. He likes English fruit desserts because they are very easy; they can be served with breakfast, lunch, or dinner; and they celebrate the seasons.

4	Gala or Golden Delicious apples
1 pint	ripe blackberries
1 cup	sugar
1 cup	water
	zest of 1 lemon
small pinch	salt

Peel the apples, core them, and cut them into eighths.

Put the apple slices in a 2-quart saucepan with all the other ingredients. Bring to a boil, reduce the heat to low, cover, and cook slowly for 10 minutes. Remove from the heat and let cool. Refrigerate, covered, until needed, for up to 2 days. Serve in a crystal bowl with your choice of cream, vanilla ice cream, or plain yogurt.

Jean-Marie Lacroix's Blackberry-Apple Compote with Lemon.

Crepes Veuve Joyeuse

PHILIPPE BOULOT

SERVES 4 TO 6

8 to 12	Dessert Crepes (page 162)
2	limes
5	egg yolks
1 cup	sugar
	salt
1/3 cup	all-purpose flour
1 cup	milk
1	vanilla bean, split lengthwise
1 tablespoon	butter
8	egg whites

I am not sure if the widow after whom this dish was named was *joyeuse*, or merry, because she ate these crepes or just because she was a widow. But I can attest to the fact that they are delicious.

Prepare the crepes as directed. Zest the limes and chop finely. Then juice the fruit and macerate the zest in the juice for 15 minutes.

Put the egg yolks, 1/3 cup of the sugar, and a pinch of salt in a bowl and whisk for 3 minutes, or until the mixture is pale yellow. Mix in the flour.

Heat the milk with the vanilla bean for 3 minutes. Gradually whisk the boiling milk and the vanilla bean into the egg yolk mixture. Transfer the custard to a saucepan and cook over medium heat, still whisking, for 3 minutes after it comes to a boil. Any lumps will disappear as you whisk. Make sure the pastry cream does not burn on the bottom at this stage. Add the lime juice and zest, mix well, and set aside to cool slightly. Remove the vanilla bean. Beat in the butter.

Whip the 8 egg whites in a bowl with the remaining 2/3 cup sugar until stiff peaks form. Fold 1/4 of the beaten whites into the cooled pastry cream, then fold the pastry cream into the remaining beaten whites.

Put a little of the soufflé mixture in the center of each crepe; fold the crepe gently in half over the filling. Arrange the filled crepes on a lightly buttered sheet pan and bake for 6 to 8 minutes, until the filling is puffed.

Serve the crepes immediately as they are, or with a little powdered sugar or your favorite dessert sauce.

Philippe Boulot's Crepes Veuve Joyeuse, served with a huckleberry sauce.

JEREMIAH TOWER

Dessert Crepes

MAKES A DOZEN
6-INCH CREPES

You will need a 6- to 7-inch
seasoned French crepe pan,
small omelet pan, or non-
stick frying pan.

1 cup	sifted all-purpose flour
1 tablespoon	confectioners' sugar
1/2 teaspoon	salt
2	eggs
1 cup	milk
4 tablespoons	melted butter
1 tablespoon	cold butter

To make the batter, put the flour, confectioners' sugar, and salt in a
bowl and mix. Add the eggs and mix well until fully incorporated.
Then stir in the milk, 1/2 cup at a time, until the mixture becomes a
smooth batter. Stir in the melted butter and let the batter sit for 1 hour
before making the crepes.

To make the crepes, put a 6- to 7-inch crepe pan over medium heat
for a minute, then add a small piece of the remaining cold butter. When
the butter is melted and sizzling, pour in 3 tablespoons of batter. Lift
the pan up and quickly tilt it in all directions to spread the batter all
over the bottom of the pan in a thin film. Pour any batter that does
not adhere in 3 to 4 seconds back into the bowl of uncooked batter.

Put the pan back on the heat for 1 minute, moving it around the flame
or burner to get even cooking. Bang the pan on the burner to loosen
the crepe and lift the edge of the crepe with a spatula or your fingers.
As soon as you see nut-colored browning on the bottom of the crepe,
turn it over either by flipping with the spatula or by dumping it out
onto a plate and then picking it up to put it back in the pan. Cook on
the second side for 30 seconds.

Put the cooked crepe on a plate and continue cooking the rest of the
batter. Stack the cooked crepes on top of one another; they can be
made several hours in advance and reheated for serving.

Crepes Suzette

PHILIPPE BOULOT

SERVES 4 TO 6

8 tablespoons	butter (1 stick)
1/3 cup	sugar
1/2 cup	freshly squeezed orange juice, strained
1/4 cup	freshly squeezed lemon juice, strained
1/4 cup	freshly squeezed lime juice, strained
1/4 cup	Grand Marnier liqueur
1 recipe	Dessert Crepes (page 162)

Put the butter and sugar in a large shallow nonstick frying pan and cook over low heat for 5 minutes, stirring to dissolve the sugar. Pour in the citrus juices and the Grand Marnier and cook for another 5 minutes.

Put 2 cooked crepes in the pan and turn them over so they are well coated with sauce. Fold them in half and put them on warm plates. Continue until all the crepes are served. Pour any remaining sauce over the crepes.

Much has been written about the origin and the authentic recipe for these Suzette French pancakes and how they were to be served. For some answers, I will go back to a debate that raged in London in the newspapers just before Escoffier died—for he was the last man to know the "truth." A French chef living in America claimed he invented them for the Prince of Wales in Monte Carlo in 1894. The very great restaurant Paillard in Paris claimed originality. Prosper Montagne of Larousse gastronomique *fame said Escoffier invented them. Two famous London French chefs working at Escoffier's previous haunts, Herbodeau (the Carlton) and Latry (the Savoy), said the origins were obscure, but Crepes Suzette had probably been created by Paillard at the 1900 Exhibition.*

Escoffier died before he could answer the riddle. But whatever the origin, Latry said that the "secret of the dish is its unctuousness and its aroma, due to the mixture of the just melted butter, sugar, and the perfume of the orange, the only one that must be represented in the Crepes Suzette." *And Suzette herself, a member of the Comedie-Francaise who had to prepare crepes on the stage in Paris in 1837, died even before Escoffier.*

There were no flames allowed then, and none now.

PATRICK O'CONNELL

SERVES 6

The tarts can be assembled well in advance and baked just before serving. Puff pastry can be used instead of the pie crust dough on page 208, if you prefer.

The Inn at Little Washington's Granny Smith Apple Tart

1 recipe	pie crust dough (page 208)
2	Granny Smith apples
3 tablespoons	unsalted butter
$1/2$ teaspoon	ground cinnamon
2 tablespoons	heavy cream
$1/3$ cup	Southern Comfort whiskey
$1/3$ cup	cinnamon sugar

On a lightly floured board, roll out the pie dough approximately $1/8$ inch thick. Turn a 5-inch mixing bowl (or other round form) upside down on the pastry and cut out circles, using up as much of the rolled-out dough as possible to get 6 rounds. Refrigerate the rounds between sheets of waxed paper.

Peel and core the apples. Cut them into $1/8$-inch slices.

Melt the butter in a large sauté pan and add the apples. Cook over medium heat for 5 minutes, stirring twice. Add the cinnamon and cream and stir again. Then add the whiskey, averting your face in case it ignites, as it will if you are using a gas stove. Continue cooking the apples until they are soft and pliable, about 10 minutes.

Remove the apples with a slotted spoon onto a nonreactive baking sheet and refrigerate until well chilled.

Simmer the cooking liquid left in the sauté pan until reduced by half. Set this mixture aside to glaze the tarts after they are baked.

Remove the pastry rounds from the refrigerator. Butter enough cookie sheets to hold the rounds and lay out the pastry on them. Place the cooked, chilled apple slices in concentric circles around the pastry, leaving a $1/4$-inch border at the edges. Roll an apple slice into a tight circle to form a rosette and place in the center of each tart. The tarts may be assembled ahead to this point and refrigerated for 1 day.

America's Best Chefs Cook *with* Jeremiah Tower

Preheat the oven to 400°F.

Dust each of the tarts with the cinnamon sugar and bake them for 7 minutes, or until the crusts are a rich golden brown. Remove the tarts from the oven and brush with the reserved cooking liquid glaze.

Being in the heart of apple-growing country, we've tried every apple dessert imaginable over the years. This is the most delicate of apple tarts. Apple slices are sautéed briefly in butter, whiskey, and cream, then arranged on thin discs of pastry and baked just before serving. A scoop of ice cream melting on top or a dollop of crème fraîche makes them even more irresistible.
—PATRICK O'CONNELL

KEN ORINGER

MAKES 6 INDIVIDUAL
CAKES

Gianduja (pronounced zhahn-*doo*-yah), refers to the combination of chocolate and hazelnuts. This is probably the best—and richest—version of the currently popular warm individual chocolate cakes that are still runny inside (the "fondant"). Ken serves them on a big white rectangular plate with a little mound of grapefruit marmalade, several small pieces of nougat broken from nougat bars he buys, a line of chopped toasted hazelnuts, and hot chocolate sauce on top of the cakes. The cakes are then topped with crème fraîche ice cream.

Ken cooks these in metal rings 3 inches in diameter and 3 inches high, but you could use 8-ounce ceramic or disposable aluminum ramekins.

Hot Gianduja "Chocolate Fondant" with Red Grapefruit Marmalade

6 ounces	Valrhona Gianduja chocolate
4 ounces	Valrhona bittersweet chocolate
10 ounces	unsalted butter (2 sticks plus 2 tablespoons), cut into pieces
2 tablespoons	unsweetened cocoa powder
4	whole eggs
4	egg yolks
1/2 cup	sugar
3/4 cup	all-purpose flour
	salt
1 recipe	Grapefruit Marmalade (recipe follows)
1/2 cup	Chocolate Sauce (recipe follows)

Preheat the oven to 400°F.

Put the chocolates in a metal bowl over barely simmering water and let melt. Add the butter and mix it in very gently. Remove the bowl from the heat and let cool slightly.

Line the bottom of six 8-ounce ramekins with a ring of parchment paper or encase the bottom and sides of 6 metal rings, 3 inches in diameter and 3 inches high, with aluminum foil. Spray with nonstick oil or brush with melted butter and then dust the interiors with cocoa powder.

Meanwhile, beat the whole eggs and egg yolks until thickened and lemon colored, about 5 minutes at high speed with a mixer. Then add the sugar and beat another 3 minutes on high speed, until the mixture is thick and pale yellow, or until the sugar is dissolved.

Add the melted chocolate to the egg mixture, stir until the chocolate is just incorporated, and then quickly and gently fold in the flour and a pinch of salt.

Pour batter into the rings or ramekins and bake on a tray in the oven for 10 minutes, until the tops of the cakes are puffed and no longer appear wet. Remove the baking sheet from the oven and let the cakes stand for 10 minutes. Use a knife to carefully loosen the cakes from the sides of the molds, then invert onto dessert plates. Garnish with the marmalade and drizzle a little chocolate sauce over each cake.

Grapefruit Marmalade

4	red grapefruits, well washed
1 cup	sugar
1 cup	water
	sea salt

MAKES ABOUT
1 1/3 CUPS

Peel the zest off the grapefruits without incorporating any of the white pith and squeeze the juice into a nonreactive saucepan. Cut the zest into strips 1/8 inch wide and 2 inches long. Put the strips in the saucepan with the juice from the grapefruits, the sugar, water, and a small pinch of salt. Bring to a boil over medium-high heat. Reduce the heat and simmer, stirring occasionally, until the zest is tender and the liquid has evaporated to a jamlike texture, about 1 hour. Let cool.

Chocolate Sauce

4 ounces	best-quality bittersweet chocolate, chopped
10 ounces	best-quality semisweet chocolate, chopped
2 tablespoons	salted butter, cut into bits
1 cup	heavy cream

JEREMIAH TOWER

MAKES 2 CUPS

Melt the bitter and semisweet chocolates and the butter in a heatproof bowl over simmering water, gently stirring occasionally. Bring the cream almost to a boil. Slowly mix the hot cream into the chocolate, stirring until smooth.

You need to treat chocolate very gently, so if melting it over water, the water must never be boiling. The longer you take to melt chocolate the nicer and smoother it will become.
—KEN ORINGER

MICHAEL ROMANO

Chocolate Pudding Flan

MAKES 6 SERVINGS

1 1/2 cups	granulated pure cane sugar
1 cup	water
3 cups	whole milk
2 tablespoons	unsweetened dark cocoa powder (Dutch process)
	salt
8 ounces	best-quality bittersweet chocolate, cut in small pieces
4	whole eggs
3	egg yolks
1 cup	whipped cream

This is a very easy version of crème caramel, but chocolate flavored. And the combination of caramel and chocolate is always sensational. Serve with sugar cookies.

You will need six 6-ounce ceramic or disposable aluminum ramekins, or you can use custard cups.

Cook 1 cup of the sugar and the water over medium-low heat until the syrup is a deep nut-colored brown. Immediately remove the caramel from the heat and, working quickly, carefully pour equal amounts into the ramekins.

Preheat the oven to 350°F.

Heat the milk in a saucepan. Stir in the remaining 1/2 cup sugar, the cocoa, and a pinch of salt until dissolved. Remove the pan from the heat, add the chocolate, and stir until melted and smooth.

Beat the whole eggs and egg yolks for a few minutes until lighter in color. Temper them by stirring in 1/2 cup of the hot chocolate milk; then pour the tempered eggs slowly into the remaining hot milk, gently whisking all the time.

Michael Romano's Chocolate Pudding Flan.

Strain the chocolate custard through a fine-mesh sieve into a heatproof glass measuring cup. Pour the chocolate mixture into the ramekins to fill them up three-quarters of the way. Put the ramekins in a baking dish or roasting pan and set in the oven. Pour enough boiling water into the dish to reach at least halfway up the ramekins. Bake until a skewer or knife inserted into the center of a pudding does not come out quite clean, 20 to 30 minutes.

Remove the puddings from the oven. Carefully transfer the ramekins to a wire rack and let cool for 5 to 10 minutes. To serve, gently run a thin knife around the edges to loosen the custard, then turn them upside down on a plate to unmold. Serve with whipped cream.

Goat's Milk Caramel with Green Apple Sorbet, Fleur de Sel, and Hazelnut Brittle

KEN ORINGER

SERVES 6

1 quart	fresh goat's milk
1 cup	sugar
1 teaspoon	baking soda
1/4 cup	ground hazelnut brittle or peanut brittle (store-bought is fine)
2	large green apples, such as Granny Smith
1 teaspoon	fleur de sel
1/2 cup	green apple sorbet

This dish is a play on caramelized apples on a stick—these are in a shot glass. Meant to be eaten from the bottom up with a small spoon, the flavors are all about the apple, and the play of sea salt against the sweetness of the goat's milk caramel, *dulce de leche*.

You will need 6 tall shot glasses.

Put the milk, sugar, and baking soda in a large saucepan and bring to a boil over medium-high heat, stirring to dissolve the sugar. Watch carefully so the mixture does not boil over. Reduce the heat to a simmer and cook, stirring occasionally, until the milk is nut brown and forms about 1 cup of thick caramel, 50 to 60 minutes. Pour into a heatproof bowl, cover, and refrigerate until cold, at least 2 hours.

Spoon 2 or 3 tablespoons of the caramel into each of the glasses to fill about 2 inches. Then spoon in half the hazelnut brittle.

Peel and core the apples; slice them 1/4 inch thick, then cut crosswise into 1/4-inch dice. Spoon the apple into the glasses, sprinkle with the fleur de sel, and then spoon in the sorbet. Finish with the remainder of the hazelnut brittle. Serve at once.

Ginger Ice Cream

CHARLIE TROTTER

SERVES 4 TO 6

2 cups	heavy cream
1/4 cup	finely chopped, peeled fresh ginger
4	egg yolks
1/4 cup	sugar
	salt

Heat the cream with the ginger to the point just before the cream boils. Let sit for 15 minutes, then strain.

Continued

Beat the egg yolks, sugar, and a pinch of salt in a bowl large enough to hold the yolks and all the cream until the sugar is dissolved and the mixture a light yellow. Slowly whisk in the cream until all of it is used and fully incorporated into the yolks.

Put the bowl over simmering water and cook until the cream and egg mixture thickens to a custard and coats the back of a spoon. The moment the custard reaches this point, put the bowl into a larger bowl filled with ice and water; stir until cold. Lift off any foam from the surface of the custard. Transfer to an ice-cream maker and freeze following the manufacturer's instructions.

CHARLIE TROTTER

MAKES 6 CAKES

You will need 6 buttered 6-ounce ramekins for these individual cakes.

Molasses Spice Cake with Quince, Burnt Orange Caramel, and Maple Mascarpone Cream

Spice Cake

2	oven-dried quinces, sliced and rolled in sugar (see Oven-Dried Pears, page 204)
1/2 cup	fresh ginger, peeled, finely chopped
3/4 cup	molasses
1/2 cup	milk
1/4 cup	freshly squeezed orange juice, strained
2 tablespoons	brandy
8 tablespoons	butter (1 stick)
1/3 cup	sugar
2	eggs, beaten
2 cups	all-purpose flour
1 1/2 teaspoons	baking soda
1/4 teaspoon	salt
1 teaspoon	ground cinnamon
1/8 teaspoon	ground cloves

Burnt orange caramel

1 cup	freshly squeezed orange juice
1 cup	sugar

Maple mascarpone cream

1 cup	mascarpone
1/2 cup	heavy cream
1/4 cup	pure maple syrup

Preheat the oven to 350°F.

Line the bottoms of six 6-ounce ramekins with the sugared, cooked quince. Mix the ginger, molasses, milk, orange juice, and brandy in a bowl.

Cream the butter and sugar in a mixer at medium speed until the sugar is dissolved and the mixture is smooth. Add the eggs and blend well.

Mix the flour, baking soda, salt, cinnamon, and cloves together in a bowl. Mix at low speed into the butter and sugar mixture, then mix in the molasses-milk until well incorporated.

Pour the batter into the ramekins and put them on a baking sheet in the oven. Bake for 15 minutes. Remove from the oven and unmold onto serving plates.

While the cakes are in the oven, make the burnt orange caramel and maple mascarpone cream: Cook the orange juice and sugar in a saucepan over medium heat until it is a dark caramel. Then, separately, mix together the mascarpone, heavy cream, and maple syrup.

Spoon the orange caramel around the warm cakes and drizzle the maple cream on top.

Charlie Trotter's Molasses Spice Cake with Quince, Burnt Orange Caramel, and Maple Mascarpone Cream.

Even without lemons right off the tree in one's backyard, this is a fast and easy, delicious dessert.

Roaring Fork's Backyard Lemon-Vodka Ice

2 cups	freshly squeezed lemon juice, strained
1³/4 cups	superfine sugar
3 cups	warm water
1/4 cup	Absolut citron vodka
1/2 cup	vodka
1	lemon

Put the lemon juice, 1 1/2 cups of the sugar, and the warm water in a bowl. Stir until the sugar is completely dissolved. Add the two vodkas and mix again.

Pour the liquid into a glass or metal loaf pan and put in the freezer.

When the liquid has started to set, break it up and mix with a fork to make sure all the alcohol is evenly distributed. Keep doing this every 20 minutes, until the mixture is entirely frozen and smooth.

Just before serving, break up the lemon ice again. Cut the lemon into 1/8-inch slices, remove any seeds, and dip both sides of each slice into the remaining 1/4 cup sugar. Scoop the lemon ice into frozen martini glasses and serve with the sugared lemon slices on the rim of the glass.

JEREMIAH TALKS ABOUT

Robert McGrath Roaring Fork, Scotsdale, Arizona

Robert McGrath barbecuing over an outdoor fire.

A LARGE PART OF WESTERN AND SOUTHWESTERN COOKING is simply attitude: relaxed, having fun. That's what Robert McGrath told me when we were cooking some enormous, "in-your-face" rib-eye steaks over an outdoor fire. For me, as for Robert, cooking outdoors is what Southwest cooking is all about—along with, McGrath added, the romance of trips down a river, building a fire, taking in the stars, and enjoying a great bottle of red wine. Robert is the kind of chef who knows that the further removed a cook or the food is from the flavors and appeal of those outdoor perfect moments, the less interesting the restaurant will be. He believes that there is no substitute for real flavors: He—and I—would rather eat one of those big, well-marbled rib-eyes, and for the rest of the month eat fish and vegetables, than settle for a lean steak of lesser quality just over worry about fat.

At Roaring Fork, it is all about Robert's philosophy on recipes: take them into your kitchen and have some fun—doing what makes culinary sense—as long as it tastes good. Roaring Fork is a unique Southwestern experience, whether waiting for a few minutes while the line forms for the happy hour hamburger and Robert opening the big wood doors, or sitting in front of the fire with a bottle of wine while watching the rose and blue colors of the desert sunlight, or tasting Robert's blend of flavors disciplined by the principles of great cooking.

"What we are really going after is robust flavor," he told me. "We are not concerned really with fancy (if that's the word), as in flavor associations and the food tasting great. Plus, it's a little down home."

Cooking with your boots on, I would call it.

ALAIN DUCASSE

SERVES 4 TO 6

Ducasse also serves this dessert with French toast made from brioche, but on the show we toasted the brioche in the oven and then dusted it with confectioners' sugar for this simpler presentation.

Brioche French Toast with Sautéed Seasonal Fruits

1/4 cup	currants
1 1/2 tablespoons	dark rum
11 tablespoons	unsalted butter (1 stick plus 3 tablespoons)
1/4 cup	granulated sugar
2	heirloom apples, peeled, cored, quartered
1	Bartlett pear, peeled, cored, quartered
1/2	small pineapple, peeled, cored, cut into 1/2-inch-thick rings
1/2	quince, peeled, cored, quartered (optional)
1	vanilla bean, halved lengthwise
4 to 6 slices	brioche, cut 3/4 inch thick
1/2 cup	confectioners' sugar
1 small bunch	white grapes, cut into bunches of 3 to 4 grapes each
1/2	orange
1/2	lemon
	salt
1 1/2 pints	rich vanilla ice cream

Preheat the oven to 400°F.

Soak the currants in the rum until they soften, about 30 minutes.

Melt 5 tablespoons of the butter in a large nonreactive skillet over medium heat. Add the granulated sugar and cook for about 2 minutes, stirring, until it begins to dissolve. Add the apples, pear, pineapple, and quince. Scrape the beans out of the vanilla pod and add the seeds and the pod to the fruit. Cook until the fruit is softened, 7 to 10 minutes, stirring from time to time with a wooden spoon or spatula.

Put the brioche slices on a baking sheet and toast in the oven until lightly browned, about 5 minutes. Remove and dust generously with the confectioners' sugar.

Add the currants and rum and the grapes to the other fruit in the pan. Squeeze the orange and lemon juice into the fruit, taking care that no seeds fall in. Add the remaining 6 tablespoons butter and a pinch of salt and simmer, stirring, until the liquid is reduced by half. Remove from the heat and set aside.

Place each slice of toasted brioche in a warmed shallow serving bowl and spoon the fruit with its juices over the toast. Top with vanilla ice cream and serve immediately.

Skillet Pecan Pie

1 recipe	pie crust dough (page 208)
3	eggs
1 cup	sugar
1 cup	corn syrup
1/3 cup	clarified butter
1/4 teaspoon	salt
1/3 cup	crumbled Heath Bar or any toffee bar
1/3 cup	pecans, very coarsely chopped
1 cup	semisweet chocolate chips
1 quart	rich vanilla ice cream

Preheat the oven to 400°F.

Line a 9-inch cast-iron skillet about 3 inches deep with the pie dough. Bake for 8 minutes, remove, and let cool. Reduce the oven temperature to 375°F.

Put the eggs, sugar, corn syrup, butter, and salt in a bowl and beat for 5 minutes. Add the toffee, pecans, and chocolate chips and mix thoroughly.

Fill the pie shell and bake in the oven for 30 to 45 minutes, or until a knife inserted into the center of the filling comes out clean. Transfer to a rack and let the pie cool for 15 minutes.

Serve with the ice cream.

ROBERT MCGRATH

SERVES 6 TO 8

Pecan pie belongs to the family of "transparent" pies based on brown sugar, molasses, and corn or maple syrup. These are either Southern or Pennsylvania Dutch, some harking back to traditional English chess tarts. My favorite is the Jefferson Davis pie, but nothing beats a really creamy pecan pie, like this one.

Robert McGrath's Skillet Pecan Pie.

NANCY SILVERTON

Meyer Lemon Curd

SERVES 4 TO 6

3	whole eggs
2	egg yolks
3/4 cup	freshly squeezed Meyer lemon juice
3/4 cup	sugar

Whisk the whole eggs and egg yolks together in a bowl for 2 minutes. Add the lemon juice and the sugar and whisk for another minute.

Put the mixture in the top of a nonreactive double boiler and cook over simmering water, stirring constantly, until thickened, 5 to 6 minutes. Remove from the heat, set the pan in the ice bath, and stir until cold. Refrigerate until firm.

While this curd recipe is so good that I use it for tarts, it is also lovely for serving with fresh berries or, as the English and French do, spreading it on brioche toast.

Using an ice bath (bowl of ice and water larger than the pan you are cooking with) is the best way to cool the curd.

—*NANCY SILVERTON*

NANCY SILVERTON

Meyer Lemon Sorbet

SERVES 4

Anyone who wants a lemon sorbet without the vodka in the Roaring Fork's Backyard Lemon-Vodka Ice (page 172) can make this one.

3 cups	freshly squeezed Meyer lemon juice
1/2 cup	corn syrup
3/4 cup	warm water
1 cup	superfine sugar
pinch	salt

Mix all the ingredients together in a bowl until the sugar is dissolved. Then put in a metal or glass loaf pan in the freezer and follow the instructions on page 172, or freeze in an ice cream maker according to the manufacturer's directions.

Hungarian Crepes
with Peanut Butter and Jam

GALE GAND

SERVES 4 TO 6

1 recipe	Dessert Crepe batter (page 162)
1/2 cup	peanut butter—smooth or chunky
1/2 cup	fruit jam (strawberry, raspberry, apricot, peach, plum, blackberry, etc.)
1/2 cup	confectioners' sugar

Preheat the oven to 200°F and put a heatproof platter in the oven to hold the crepes as they are cooked.

Cook the crepes as on page 162, storing them in the warm oven as you make them. When all of them are cooked, remove the stack from the oven. One by one, spread each crepe with a thin layer of peanut butter and jam and roll up like a cigar. Place 2 rolled crepes on each of 4 or 6 serving plates. Sprinkle with confectioners' sugar and serve with a tall glass of ice-cold milk.

Recipes from previous generations are a great way for children who never met their grandparents to get to know them.
—GALE GAND

Jeremiah in the kitchen with Gale's son, Giorgio.

Gale's mother Myrna always had a terrific knack for pastry. Instead of a green thumb for gardening, she used to say that she and Gale had a white thumb for baking: "Many of Myrna's specialties have their roots in Hungary, where her family came from, and where fine baking has a long, long tradition. Crepes, like these *palscintas*, are popular all over Eastern Europe, usually spread with the region's famous fruit compotes and jams. Adding peanut butter makes them all-American and kid friendly."

When I cooked with Gale's five-year-old son, Giorgio, he made some crepes stuffed just with whipped cream and then dusted with sugar. I think those were Grandma Myrna's.

Pear, Red Wine, and Basil Upside-Down Tart

SERVES 4 TO 6

This tart is basically a "Tarte Tatin" using pears cooked in red wine and basil instead of apples. I serve this with caramel ice cream.

6	pears, all the same size, slightly under-ripe
1 bottle	red wine, like a young zinfandel
3/4 cup	sugar
1 piece	freshly cut lemon zest, 2 inches by 1/2 inch
8 leaves	fresh basil
	salt and freshly ground white pepper
4 tablespoons	unsalted butter, softened
1 recipe	tart shell pastry (page 208)

Peel the pears, cut them in half lengthwise, and core them. Save the peelings.

Heat the wine, sugar, and lemon zest in a nonreactive saucepan large enough to hold the liquid and all the pear halves. Add the pears and the peelings; simmer until the pears are just tender when poked in the thickest part with a toothpick or skewer, 20 to 30 minutes. Remove the pears from the liquid, cover with a damp towel, and let cool.

Strain the wine, discarding the peelings. Boil the wine until it is reduced by half, thick, and syrupy. Stir in the basil leaves (making sure you submerge them immediately) and a pinch of salt and white pepper; let cool.

Generously grease a round cast-iron skillet or tarte tatin pan just large enough to hold the pears with the butter. Arrange the pears in the dish like the spokes of a wheel, with the thick ends at the outer edge of the dish and the stem ends pointing toward the center. Pour the cooled syrup over the pears.

Preheat the oven to 375°F.

Roll out the pastry to a circle about 1/4 inch less than the circumference of the dish. Place the pastry on top of the pears. Bake in the oven until the pastry is golden and cooked through, about 20 minutes.

Let the tart cool for 15 minutes. If the juices are still watery, cook the tart on the stovetop over high heat until the juices are sputtering and thickened. Wait 5 minutes, then place a platter on top of the pan, and invert the whole thing so that the pears are on top of the tart.

Jeremiah's Pear, Red Wine, and Basil Upside-Down Tart.

Trio's Individual Apple Tarts

GALE GAND

1 sheet	frozen puff pastry, thawed slowly in the refrigerator
4	Granny Smith apples, peeled, halved, cored
1/2 cup plus 4 teaspoons	sugar
1/4 teaspoon	cinnamon
pinch	salt
4 tablespoons	butter, cut into 16 cubes

SERVES 8

By all means, buy puff pastry already made, as long as it is made with butter.

On a lightly floured work surface, roll out the puff pastry a little thinner than 1/8 inch. Lay the pastry out on a sheet pan or a large cookie sheet and refrigerate for 15 minutes.

Slice the apples very thinly, preferably on a mandoline or Japanese vegetable cutter.

In a small bowl mix the sugar, cinnamon, and salt together.

Preheat the oven to 375°F.

Cut out eight 4-inch rounds from the chilled pastry. Lay them on a parchment paper–lined sheet or cookie pan. Place 1 cube of butter and 1 teaspoon cinnamon sugar in the center of each round.

Start layering and stacking the apple slices in concentric circles on each pastry round, leaving very little edge showing, to make a beehive shape; save the smaller pieces for the top layers. The shape should get smaller as you go up higher, and when you are finished the stack should be about 3 inches high. Place a cube of butter at the top and sprinkle the apple stack liberally with cinnamon sugar. You can freeze the tarts at this point.

Bake in the oven until golden brown, about 30 minutes.

I learned how to make these from Nico Landanis, a 3-star Michelin chef with whom I spent time in his London kitchen. He made these tarts ahead of time, froze them, and then baked them to order.

—GALE GAND

Gale Gand's Individual Apple Tart.

Hickory Nut Strudel

3 cups	toasted hickory nuts, pecans, or hazelnuts
2 3/4 cups	heavy cream
1 1/2 cups	maple syrup
	salt
1 cup	sugar
12 sheets	fresh phyllo dough
1 cup	warm melted butter

This dish, Odessa says, is for the late winter and early spring when the maple syrup runs. And she particularly loves the hickory nut. You could use pecans or hazelnuts here, but the strudel would not have that haunting flavor that only hickories have.

Odessa says that phyllo dough can smell your fear—and it will, if you don't follow Odessa's method of handling it, which even I managed to do, and I am not a pastry person. Odessa used 8 sheets of phyllo, then another to wrap the strudel. You may need the other 3 I call for if a couple have holes in them. You will also need a 2- to 3-inch-wide clean pastry brush.

To make the filling, put 2 cups of the nuts, 2 cups of the cream, 1 cup of the maple syrup, and a pinch of salt in a heavy saucepan. Cook over low heat until the cream is greatly reduced and the nut mass is the consistency of bread dough. For the last 10 minutes, stir continuously so that the nuts and cream do not burn. Let the nut cream cool to lukewarm.

Make the strudel: Put the remaining 1 cup nuts, the sugar, and a pinch of salt in a food processor. Pulse to puree the nuts only to the point at which they are 1/8-inch nuggets. Do not overprocess to a paste.

Lay out a sheet of phyllo on parchment paper larger than the sheet of dough and paint the edges of the dough with the warm melted butter. Then paint the whole sheet. Sprinkle with the nut-sugar mix. Then lay another sheet on top of that, paint the edges with more butter, sprinkle with the nut-sugar mix, and keep going until you have used up 8 sheets of phyllo. With each sheet, start 1 inch from the previous edge in the direction away from you, so that when the strudel is folded up, the edge will hold together better. Then spread the nut cream evenly over the final sheet, keeping the filling 1 inch away from the edges.

Roll the strudel up away from you as tightly as possible, as you would a jelly roll, continuing to butter as you roll. Put aside for a moment with the edge side down and paint a final sheet with butter. Put the roll inside this sheet with the edges down and roll up again, continuing to butter as you roll, so that the ragged seam edge is rolled up inside the new sheet, and you have only one seam.

Preheat the oven to 400°F.

Odessa Piper's Hickory Nut Strudel, topped with whipped cream, hazelnuts, and maple syrup.

Let the roll cool, then cut it into 1/2-inch-thick slices. Put the slices on parchment paper on a cookie sheet and bake for 10 minutes. Reduce the oven temperature to 350°F, brush the slices with the remaining melted butter, and bake them for another 10 minutes, or until they are cooked and flaky throughout.

Serve while still warm, half-covered with whipped cream, a drizzle of maple syrup, and more chopped hazelnuts, if you like.

Oven-Dried Quinces in Hibiscus Soup

1/2 cup	dried hibiscus flowers
1 cup	simple syrup (see page 55)
	salt
1/2 cup	superfine sugar
1 sprig	fresh rosemary, stemmed, leaves finely chopped
1	large pink-yellow rose
4	Oven-Dried Quinces (see Oven-Dried Pears, page 204), peeled, halved (into quarters)
1/2 cup	cold Dessert Custard Sauce (recipe follows)

Put the hibiscus flowers in the syrup, add a pinch of salt, and heat (but not to a boil) for a few minutes. Remove from the heat and let steep for 30 minutes. Strain and chill the liquid.

Mix the sugar and the rosemary. Cut the rose petals into fine shreds and mix into the rosemary sugar. Let sit for 30 minutes.

Put the pieces of quince in chilled large white soup plates. Then pour or spoon the hibiscus flower soup around them. Drizzle some of the custard over the quince and around the soup. Then lift the rose shreds out of the sugar and garnish the quince with them.

JEREMIAH TOWER

SERVES 4

This was a dish that I invented after nosing around Charlie Trotter's preparations for cooking on the show and noticing that he was going to use one of my favorite foodstuffs—ripe quinces. Then I was served a cup of hibiscus tea, and an idea for an unconventional soup sprang into my mind.

There was some sweetened, fresh blackberry puree on hand in Charlie's kitchen, so I drizzled that around the dish as a final touch.

Jeremiah's Oven-Dried Quinces in Hibiscus Soup with a swirl of Dessert Custard Sauce.

Dessert Custard Sauce

SERVES 4 TO 6
MAKES ABOUT 3 CUPS

This is the sauce called
"crème Anglaise" in French.

1/2 cup	sugar
6	egg yolks
1/4 teaspoon	salt
2 cups	milk
1-inch piece	vanilla bean

Mix the sugar, yolks, and salt in a bowl and whisk (or use a mixer on medium speed) until pale yellow, 3 to 5 minutes.

Prepare an ice bath with a bowl sitting in the iced water.

Heat the milk and vanilla bean together until almost boiling. Slowly whisk the egg yolk mixture into the hot vanilla milk. Transfer to a double boiler and cook over simmering water, stirring constantly, until the custard begins to thicken and coats the spoon.

Remove from heat and pour into the bowl sitting in the ice. Stir constantly with a spoon to prevent the custard from overcooking (curdling) and forming a skin when it cools. Strain and serve, or cover and refrigerate for up to 3 days.

America's Best Chefs Cook *with* Jeremiah Tower

Shortbread Buttons

NANCY SILVERTON

MAKES ABOUT
24 COOKIES

8 tablespoons	unsalted butter (1 stick)
1/4 cup	brown sugar
1/4 teaspoon	salt
13/4 cups	pastry flour, sifted
1/4 cup	bread flour, sifted
1/4 cup	all-purpose flour, sifted, for dusting board

Preheat the oven to 250°F.

Put the butter, brown sugar, and salt in the bowl of an electric mixer with a paddle attachment and beat on medium speed for 10 minutes.

Add the sifted pastry and bread flours, and mix until combined. Scrape down the bowl and the paddle, and mix again briefly.

Roll out on a well-floured board until 1/2 inch thick. Cut into either 21/2-inch fluted circles or into 11/2- by 4 inch bars.

Put the shortbread on cookie sheets and bake in the oven until caramelized, about 2 hours.

Nancy Silverton's Shortbread Buttons and Meyer Lemon Sorbet.

MICHAEL ROMANO

Peanut Butter Cookies

MAKES 3¹/₂ TO 4 DOZEN
2-INCH COOKIES

1 cup	smooth peanut butter
¹/₂ cup	corn oil
1	large egg
¹/₂ teaspoon	vanilla extract
¹/₂ cup	granulated sugar
1 cup	all-purpose flour
¹/₂ teaspoon	baking soda
¹/₂ cup	confectioners' sugar
¹/₂ teaspoon	salt
1 cup	plain, roasted peanuts, very coarsely chopped

These are wonderful
cookies—very rich, easy,
and quick to make.

Preheat the oven to 350°F.

In a mixing bowl, combine the peanut butter, corn oil, egg, vanilla,
and granulated sugar. Beat until smooth and blended.

Meanwhile, in another bowl, mix together the flour, baking soda, confectioners' sugar, and salt. Whisk gently to blend. Stir in the peanuts.
Gradually add the flour mixture to the peanut butter mixture, working
the dough only until it comes together. Do not overmix.

Drop the dough by heaping tablespoons onto a parchment-paper-
covered baking sheet. Bake for 15 to 18 minutes, or until the cookies
are very light golden brown on the bottom. Let rest on the baking
sheet for 2 minutes, then transfer to wire racks to cool completely.

**Michael Romano's Peanut Butter
Cookies**

Trio's Mint Chocolate-Chip Meringues

1/2 cup	egg whites (from 4 large eggs)
2/3 cup	sugar
1/2 teaspoon	pure mint extract (*not* mint oil)
2 ounces	unsweetened chocolate, finely chopped or grated
2 ounces	semisweet chocolate

GALE GAND

MAKES ABOUT 90 TINY
MERINGUES

Preheat the oven to 325°F. Warm the egg whites and sugar in a mixer bowl set over barely simmering water until warm to the touch—this will get more air into the whites when you whip them. Beat the whites on a mixer with the whip attachment until soft peaks form. Add the mint extract and continue whipping just until stiff and glossy. Fold in the chopped unsweetened chocolate. Fill a pastry bag, fitted with a large plain or star tip, with the mixture. Pipe bite-sized "kisses" onto 2 cookie sheets lined with parchment paper or nonstick baking mats.

Bake until the meringues are the color of milky coffee, 25 to 30 minutes. To test, remove one meringue from the oven, let cool 1 minute, then taste: it should be dry and crisp all the way through. Let cool on the pans.

Melt the semisweet chocolate. Dip the tines of a fork into the chocolate and drizzle melted chocolate over the meringues until they are about half covered in very thin lines of chocolate. Let the chocolate set for 30 to 45 minutes, or set in the refrigerator for 15 minutes. Store in an airtight container for up to 3 days.

Meringues are an absolute classic in the grand tradition of petit fours. *But you'll never see a mint chocolate-chip meringue on a French pastry tray—it's a completely American flavor combination, and one that I love. In this easy, superlight cookie, I use shards of unsweetened chocolate and a sweet meringue mixture for a great contrast.*

These meringues do have the melting texture of the French original, but don't expect the bright green color of American mint chocolate-chip ice cream! The finished meringues are a pale cappuccino color when baked, and will be dry and crisp all the way through to the center.

—GALE GAND

Gale Gand's Mint Chocolate-Chip Meringues.

JEREMIAH TALKS ABOUT
Gale Gand TRU, Chicago

I HAD NEVER MET GALE GAND BEFORE I WALKED INTO HER RESTAURANT TRU IN CHICAGO, which she runs with partner Rick Tramonto. So I did not know what to expect, especially since she said we would be cooking several dishes with her five-year-old son, Giorgio, and especially since one of the dishes was to be a root beer float. I knew we were in playful territory when, right at the outset, she told me, "The most important part of a root beer float is an elbow straw," and that "if you are living in a country where you can't get root beer, get a root beer–colored dog."

But it was serious play as I entered TRU and marveled at the artwork. Very few restaurant dining rooms can use important art to create an atmosphere that is inspiring without making such a strong statement that all conversations stop and appetites flag. At TRU, all is in balance, and I should have known immediately that the root beer was part of that balance. TRU's beautiful artwork was not so much to be taken "seriously" as to be enjoyed, and that is how the food is served. My favorite presentations were the Fish and Chips (seviche in a bowl, perched in another bowl in which a Siamese fighting fish is swimming— "don't worry, they work union hours," I was told) and the Caviar Stairway to Heaven, a series of steps cut out of thick glass that reminded me of a Fred Astaire and Ginger Rogers MGM musical dance set.

A lot of the balance in TRU obviously comes from Gale's common-sense style, rooted in family cooking that allows no time or space to fool around. "I use store-bought puff pastry. I don't have time for all those turns and there is such good-quality pastry out there now," she said. Coming from a pastry chef, these words were all the more commendable in my eyes, especially since I had believed this for years but had never had the sense to admit it. Gale then told me why she taught her son to cook and why she chose certain recipes for him.

"Recipes from the previous generations are a great way for the children who never met their grandparents to get to know them," she said.

Recipes like her grandmother's crepes: Judging from the way Giorgio made the batter, heated the buttered pans, tilted the batter around (tipping out the excess), and rolled up the finished crepes, I sensed that his grandmother was sitting on his shoulder, looking on, and beaming with approval.

At least that is how I felt, as I pulled away from the house in a late afternoon ice storm. It was bleak outside, but the van was filled with the perfume of still-warm cookies and just-baked chocolate meringues. Those smells and the memory of several generations of family love made the ice outside seem safely far away.

Gale Gand and Jeremiah making crepes with Gale's son, Giorgio.

Persimmon and Chestnut Tender Biscotti

MAKES ABOUT
20 BISCOTTI

These are not hard biscotti, but more cakelike. At her restaurant L'Etoile, Odessa Piper serves them with the Banon-style cheeses from Capriole farm at the corner of Indiana and Kentucky, where she thinks some of the greatest American cheeses come from. Banon-style cheeses are made from the first milk of the spring, and the wrapping leaves are chestnut, though dipped in Kentucky bourbon, not the marc that is used in France.

6 tablespoons	unsalted butter
2 1/2 cups	sugar
4	large eggs
1 tablespoon	freshly grated orange zest
1 cup	organic, sulphur-free, dried persimmons, chopped
2 cups	peeled, cooked chestnuts—1 cup chopped, 1 cup left whole
1 teaspoon	cider vinegar
2 tablespoons	bourbon
6 cups	all-purpose flour
2 teaspoons	toasted anise seeds, ground
1 tablespoon	baking powder
1 teaspoon	salt
2	Banon-style goat cheeses wrapped in chestnut leaves
8 ounces	15-year-old single-cask bourbon whiskey

Preheat the oven to 350°F. Line a cookie sheet with parchment paper.

Beat the butter in an electric mixer with a paddle attachment until creamy, about 5 minutes. Gradually add the sugar and continue beating until the mixture is light and fluffy. Then beat in the eggs one at a time until fully incorporated. Add the orange zest, persimmons, chopped chestnuts, vinegar, and bourbon. Turn the machine to low speed and add half the flour. While it is mixing, put the anise seeds, baking powder, salt, and 2 tablespoons of the flour in a little bowl and mix together; add to the dough. Add enough of the remaining flour to form a soft dough that comes together but is still sticky. Add the rest of the flour, if necessary.

Turn the dough out onto a floured board, flatten it out, and spread the whole chestnuts over the surface. With floured hands, fold the dough over to incorporate and mix in the chestnuts. Roll the dough into a log, and put it on the cookie sheet.

Bake in the oven for 30 minutes, or until the top of the roll is golden and springy. Take the roll out and let cool. Leave the oven on.

Odessa Piper's Persimmon and Chestnut Tender Biscotti.

To serve, cut the Banon cheeses into wedges with the leaves still on and put on a large plate. Slice the biscotti roll into 1/2-inch-thick slices and warm the slices in the oven for a couple of minutes, then place some on each plate. Pour the bourbon into small glasses. The idea is to spread the cheese on the biscotti and eat them while sipping the old, single-cask bourbon.

Caramel Boings

GALE GAND

MAKES 40 BOINGS

2 cups	sugar
1/2 cup	water
1 tablespoon	vegetable oil

These take about 15 minutes to prepare and 15 minutes to make. You will need a sharpening steel and parchment paper in an airtight container with a lid, and a bowl of iced water.

Put the sugar in a 1-quart saucepan. Pour the water down around the walls of the pan carefully so that no water or sugar splashes up. Draw your finger through the sugar in an X to let the water infiltrate the sugar completely. Bring the water to a boil and continue to cook over medium heat without stirring until the syrup is amber colored. Test the color of the caramel periodically by placing a drop on a white plate.

Meanwhile, very lightly wipe the sharpening steel with the vegetable oil.

Continued

Whimsy on the plate: Gale Gand's Caramel Boings.

When the caramel is slightly lighter than you want—nut colored—stop the cooking by placing the bottom of the saucepan in a bowl of ice water. Swirl the caramel a bit to cool it evenly. When the caramel has cooled enough to slowly fall from a spoon, gather up about a tablespoon in a dessert spoon and hold it over the saucepan. Let the caramel drop and, once you have a strand falling from the spoon, hold the sharpening steel over the saucepan and wind the caramel around and around the oiled steel to form a spring shape. When you reach the end of the steel, pinch the end of the caramel to cut it off.

Let the coil cool for 30 seconds, then slide it off the steel. Place the coils in an airtight container with folded parchment paper between the boings.

> *Sugar in a crystalline form is its natural way to be, and we are trying to talk it into changing that form, into being a liquid. I never bother to wash down the sides while the sugar is cooking—just make sure the edges are clean of sugar crystals to begin with.*
>
> —GALE GAND

Basic Recipes

White Chicken Stock

MAKES 5 TO 6 QUARTS

5 pounds	chicken or duck parts—backs, wings, feet, necks
5 quarts	water
1	large onion, peeled, chopped
1	large carrot, peeled, chopped
3 stalks	celery, washed, chopped
1	large Herb Bundle (page 210)
2 tablespoons	salt

Chop the vegetables in 1-inch pieces (halfway in size between fish and veal/beef), since the poultry stocks cook for only 2 hours, and the vegetables must cook and fall apart in that time.

For a clear stock, bring the liquid to a boil quickly, but be there when it first boils, because you have to immediately turn it down to a mere simmer. That initial boiling will release albumin and blood, which rise to the surface of the water. Skim that all off until there is none left, and with the occasional gentle stirring in the first 10 minutes, the stock will be crystal clear.

Old boiling hens will give the best stock (and meat for salad), but bones, feet (for gelatinous structure in the stock, important for sauces), and parts are the most economical.

Rinse and wash the chicken parts under cold running water. It is important to wash away any blood so that the stock, free of blood and albumins, stands the best chance of being clear when it is finished.

Put the chicken parts in a pot with the water. Bring to a boil over high heat. The moment it boils, lower the heat to a bare simmer. Skim off all the scum and fat on the surface of the water. Gently move the bones around a bit to loosen more blood and albumin, then skim again. Keep skimming and stirring until the stock is clear.

When the stock is clear, add the vegetables, herb bundle, and salt, and simmer, uncovered, for 2 hours. Strain the stock, cool uncovered quickly, and refrigerate, covered, until needed.

For rich stock, simmer the strained stock until reduced by one third.

Quick Chicken Stock

For a quick stock, just simmer some chicken wings in the same way as the recipe for chicken stock, and you will have a delicious stock in 20 minutes (with the bonus of having the best part of the chicken to eat). The wings actually make a good stock even without the vegetables and herbs.

Rich Brown Chicken Stock

Use bones and chicken cooked in the oven until browned, and use chicken stock instead of water. Deglaze the roasting pan with stock after the chicken is browned, pour the resulting liquid over the bones, and cook as for white chicken stock. After the stock is strained and the fat removed, reduce by one-third or a half depending on the strength called for.

Vegetable Stock

1	large onion, peeled, chopped
1	large carrot, peeled, chopped
1	leek, chopped, washed
1 stalk	celery, chopped
1	bay leaf
1 sprig	fresh thyme
2 sprigs	fresh parsley
1 tablespoon	salt
4 quarts	cold water
1 cup	dry white wine

Put the vegetables, herbs, and salt in a pot with the water. Bring to a boil, skim, and simmer, uncovered, for 20 minutes.

Add the wine and simmer for another 20 minutes.

Strain through a fine-mesh sieve into a bowl, discarding the vegetables, and let cool. Store in the refrigerator for no more than 2 days, or freeze in covered containers for up to 1 month.

JEREMIAH TOWER

MAKES 3 TO 4 QUARTS

This aromatic broth is a poaching liquid for fish, shellfish, and vegetables. The wine is added halfway through, because, if added at the start, the acid in the wine would prevent the vegetables from cooking and giving up their flavor to the broth.

You can use a food processor to chop up the vegetables into 1/4-inch pieces, though I would cut the onions by hand. This is less work—and allows maximum contact between the water and vegetables, ensuring the shortest cooking time and keeping the freshest possible flavors.

Boiled Lobster
Par-Boiled Lobster to Be Reheated

To kill the lobsters, cut deeply 1 inch behind the eyes. Put the lobsters in a pot and pour in enough cold water to cover them by 6 inches. Turn the heat on high and cook until just before the water boils. Turn off the heat and let the lobsters sit in the hot water according to the times below. Remove the lobsters, put in a colander, and cover with ice so they cool down and stop cooking.

1-pound lobsters: 1 minute

2-pound lobsters: 3 minutes

3-pound lobsters: 4 minutes

The meat yield will depend on the time of year and the thickness of the shell, but generally, from a 1-pound lobster the yield is 6 to 8 ounces; from a 2-pound lobster, 18 to 20 ounces; and from a 3-pound lobster, $1^{1}/2$ pounds.

TO REMOVE THE LOBSTER MEAT

While taking the lobster apart and getting the meat out of the shell, work over a bowl so that you save all those very flavorful juices. As you remove each part of the meat, put it on a large plate or platter so that all the pieces lie flat and separate from each other. Save all the shells for soup, sauces, and fish and shellfish stews; if not using them right away, seal them in heavy-duty plastic and freeze.

First, twist off the small legs, cutting off and discarding bits of feathery gill bits sticking to the knuckle ends. Keep the legs on the platter with the lobster meat.

Twist off the two claw arms and twist off the claws. Put the claws back in the water for 5 to 10 minutes, depending on the size of the lobster. With a pair of scissors or poultry shears, cut down the length of the (knuckle) arms, and pull out the meat.

Twist off the flaps at the end of the tail and reserve (big ones have wonderfully juicy lobster meat inside). Twist off the tail and cut through the soft shell on the underside of the tail with a knife or scissors, being careful to cut only the shell and not the tail meat. Hold the tail in both hands on the table and break it open. Lift out the meat. Make a 1/8-inch-deep cut down the center of the outside curve of the tail meat and pick out the intestinal tract.

Remove the claws and gently crack them with a mallet. Move the small lower part of the claw around and slowly pull it away from the larger part of the claw. With luck, it will come away and leave the thin meat of the little claw intact. Now all you have to do is get the big shell off the meat, so very gently pull out, cut out, shake out, or lift out the claw meat in one piece, if possible. If the lobster is in a soft-shell stage, you can use scissors to cut away all the shells from the lobster meat.

Lift the main shell (the curved top with eyes and feelers) off the central body of the lobster; scoop out any of the white fat clinging to the shell and reserve it for sauces. Remove the mouth sac at the head of the shell and discard. Scoop out any dark green eggs (if the lobster is female) and the liver or tomalley (green in both males and females), and reserve for sauces. Keep the shell either for stock or for display. The white main body part has the feathery lungs, so remove those and discard. Rinse off what is left and save for lobster or shellfish broth.

MAKES 1 GALLON

Despite what most cookbooks tell you, fish stocks should be brought to a boil as fast as possible, so that all the albumin coagulates and rises to the surface for skimming.

Simmer for no more than 30 minutes, or the stock will taste "fishy" and stale.

The vegetables have to be small so that they cook entirely in this short time, and the acid from the wine is necessary if you are to use the stock for making butter sauces, but it is added only after the vegetables have given up most of their flavor (it would impede this process if added at the beginning).

Any leftover stock can be frozen for up to a month.

Fish Stock

5 pounds	fish carcasses
1 cup	finely chopped celery
1 cup	finely chopped onion
2	bay leaves
1 sprig	fresh thyme or $1/2$ teaspoon dried leaves
2 sprigs	fresh parsley
1 sprig	fresh tarragon or chervil, or $1/2$ teaspoon dried leaves
$1^{1}/2$ teaspoons	salt
4 quarts	cold water
1 cup	dry white wine

Wash the fish carcasses, removing the gills from the heads and scraping away, under running water, any blood from the backbone.

Put the celery, onion, herbs, and salt in a pot. Add 1 cup of the water, cover, and sweat the mixture over low heat for 10 minutes. Do not let any browning occur.

Add the fish carcasses and remaining water. Bring to a boil over high heat. The moment it boils, lower the heat to a bare simmer. Stir the bones around very gently for a few seconds so that any coagulated albumin trapped at the bottom will rise to the surface. Skim any scum off the surface, avoiding any floating vegetables or herbs. Simmer, uncovered, for 20 minutes.

Add the wine and simmer for another 10 minutes. Remove from the heat, let sit for 5 minutes, then carefully ladle all the stock into a fine strainer over a container. Do not press down on any fish in the strainer. Pour off the last of the stock into the strainer and discard the debris. Immediately refrigerate the stock, uncovered. When it is cold, cover and refrigerate until needed.

Tip: The best fish to use in a light stock for cream and butter sauces are sole, turbot, halibut, and trout. For fish soups and hearty stews, use whatever non-oily fish bones and heads you have: bass, grouper, snapper, haddock, etc.

Quick Shellfish Stock

2 pounds	fresh mussels, washed
3 cups	fish stock or 1 cup clam broth and 2 cups water
2 sprigs	fresh thyme
2 sprigs	fresh parsley
1/2 cup	dry white wine

Put all the ingredients in a pot, cover, and bring to a boil over high heat. Cook for 10 minutes and strain. Decant the strained stock into another container, leaving 1/8 inch of the old behind along with its sand.

JEREMIAH TOWER

MAKES 3 TO 4 CUPS

Fresh mussels are the way to a 10-minute, rich shellfish stock. Pour either fish stock or bottled clam juice and water over them, add a little white wine and fresh herbs, and there you have it—a fine, flavorful stock as well as the mussels, which can be used for a salad, as a hot first course, or chopped up and folded into mayonnaise as a sauce for grilled fish.

Lobster (Shellfish) Stock

4 cups	lobster shells (from 3 lobsters)
4 cups	fish stock (page 196)
4 tablespoons	unsalted butter
1/4 cup	dry white wine

Smash up the lobster shells and simmer with the fish stock and butter for 15 minutes. Add the wine and simmer for another 20 minutes. Strain, discarding the shells; cool the stock and put in the refrigerator. When the stock is cold, lift the lobster butter off the top of the stock and use for recipes calling for it.

JEREMIAH TOWER

MAKES 4 CUPS

This recipe works for lobster, shrimp, or prawn shells (crab shells don't give up much flavor or color and are usually too hard to process).

Tossing raw shells in hot olive or canola oil in a frying pan for a few minutes to turn them red is passable, but I hate the flavor the shells tend to get (with the inevitable overcooking) in the oven. Boiled shells give a much subtler flavor.

If the shells are not cooked, steam them covered in a little stock or toss them in hot oil for 5 minutes over medium heat.

Lobster or Shellfish Essence

Essences are good in cream sauces or for mixing with lemon juice and oils for salad dressing. They are also useful when reduced and mixed with butter to make a shellfish butter.

If using prawn shells, grind the shells in a food processor just enough to break them up. If using lobster shells, just put them in a bowl of an electric mixer fitted with the dough hook or paddle and turn the mixer on to the lowest speed possible for 15 minutes. Wrap some aluminum foil around the top of the bowl and the mixer arm to keep the lobster shells from jumping out of the bowl as they are crushed. Add 1 cup of the stock, turn the speed up one notch, and mix for another 10 minutes.

Add the remaining fish stock and mix on low speed until the shells are completely broken up in small pieces and the stock in the bowl is red colored, about another 15 minutes. (The long mixing time is necessary to break up the shells gradually and extract the full flavor and color.)

Scrape all the shells and any essence sticking to the sides of the bowl into a saucepan. Strain completely, pressing down on the shells, reserving the liquid and discarding the shells. Refrigerate for up to 2 days or freeze for up to a month.

Shellfish Butter

Use the same method as for shellfish essence, but add 1 pound of room-temperature butter in the last 30 minutes of processing the shells in the mixer. Cook the shells only 5 minutes, strain, and refrigerate the liquid. When it is cold, lift off the butter from the top and use it to enrich sauces, or season it and put it on grilled fish.

This butter freezes well and will hold for a month in the freezer.

America's Best Chefs Cook *with* Jeremiah Tower

Veal Stock

5 pounds	veal shank bones, feet, and scraps
1	pig or veal foot
5 quarts	water
4 cups	Aromatic Vegetable Mix (page 207)
1	Herb Bundle (page 210)
1 tablespoon	salt

Put the veal and foot in a large stockpot that will hold the meat and twice as much water as meat, which should be covered by 6 inches.

Bring the water to a simmer while you skim off any scum; gently move the bones around and skim again, all this for about 45 minutes. As soon as the water simmers, turn off the heat, and let the pot sit for 5 minutes.

Drain the bones and meat in a colander and run cold water over them to completely clean them of any scum, which, if left, would result in a cloudy and gray stock that will never have any clarity of taste.

Clean the pot and return it to the stove. Put the bones back in and cover with water (or stock if you are doing a double stock), going through the same procedure as the first simmer, scum and prodding. The moment it simmers, it should be clear. Turn the heat down to low, add the vegetable mix, the herb bundle, and salt. Simmer gently for 4 hours. Turn off the heat and let the stock sit for 15 minutes to let any solids fall to the bottom.

Ladle the stock into a sieve lined with cheesecloth (or through a very fine strainer) into a container large enough to hold it (another pot, perhaps). Strain the last few inches of stock at the bottom of the pot into another container in case it has solids in it that would cloud the stock. If it does not, then add it to the main body of the stock.

Let the stock cool and then immediately refrigerate, uncovered, until it is cold. Cover and keep for up to 2 days or freeze in 1- or 2-cup containers for later use.

JEREMIAH TOWER

MAKES ABOUT 3 QUARTS

The taste of veal stock does not have much character, but the gelatinous structure of veal stock does give body to all the other stocks of meats and poultry and, therefore, to the finished sauces made from them. Without veal you have to use a lot of chicken wings, beef shanks, and even pigs' feet to get the same kind of gelatinous structure in the stocks.

Since good veal bones are not always available, I often use parboiled pork skin or pig feet (after the trotters are cooked you can eat them grilled with lots of mustard). For a full beef flavor, use oxtail (also delicious after it is cooked, breaded, and baked). Beef shin gives the most body to the stock, but half shin and half chuck works as well.

When you use veal bones and meat in a white stock, it is important to rinse them off, put them in cold water, and bring to a boil. Then dump the bones and meat into the sink—and wash all that dirty water down the drain. Finally, rinse the veal in running cold water again.

Put the bones into a clean pot and cook for 6 hours, with the usual constant skimming and a little bit of gentle prodding in the first 30 minutes. Only this way can you be guaranteed a clear stock.

For brown stock, roast the bones 45 minutes in the oven and follow the procedure as in lamb stock.

ALAIN DUCASSE

MAKES 5 CUPS

This recipe is adapted from Alain Ducasse's *Flavors of France* to support the recipes from the show. The original recipe has these notes: "This jus is virtually a sauce, the essence of veal, smothered with butter." The butter will harden on top of the jus when chilled and act as a seal, keeping the air out; remove the butter before using the jus.

Beef Stock

If using beef bones, it is not a bad idea to follow the procedure as in veal stock. If using meat scraps, then follow the procedure without the initial simmer and washing.

Quick Beef Stock

Use hamburger meat instead of beef scraps and/or bones. And cut the vegetables smaller, since you have to cook this stock only 1 hour.

Beef or Veal Jus

3 tablespoons	olive oil (not extra virgin)
$1/2$ pound	unsalted butter (2 sticks)
$4^1/2$ pounds	meaty beef or veal scraps and trimmings (or inexpensive veal cut into 1-inch cubes)
3	medium carrots
6 stems	fresh parsley
1 stalk	celery, cut in 3-inch pieces
1 head	garlic, cut in half through the equator
1 tablespoon	fine sea salt
$1/2$ teaspoon	freshly ground pepper

Heat the oil in a large stockpot over medium-high heat. Add 10 tablespoons of the butter and let it melt. Add the meat scraps and stir with a wooden spoon to coat all the pieces with the oil and butter. Then add the carrots, parsley, celery, garlic, salt, and pepper. Cook, stirring frequently, until the meat is well browned all over. Remove the meat and vegetables from the pot with a slotted spoon and set aside.

Add 1 cup of water to the pot and scrape up all the browned bits from the bottom of the pot. Boil until almost all the water evaporates.

Return the meat and the vegetables to the stockpot and add enough water to cover by at least 2 inches. Bring to a boil over high heat, reduce the heat to medium, and simmer for 3 hours, stirring gently from time to time.

America's Best Chefs Cook with Jeremiah Tower

Add the remaining 6 tablespoons butter to the stock and stir until melted. With a slotted spoon, remove the meat and vegetables and discard. Strain the stock through a strainer lined with cheesecloth into a large clean pot.

Bring the stock to a boil, reduce the heat to medium-high so that it boils gently, and cook until it reduces by half to about 5 cups, about 20 minutes.

Pour into a bowl or other storage container and let cool. Store in the refrigerator for up to 3 days, or transfer to several small containers and freeze.

Meat Jus

NANCY OAKES

MAKES ABOUT 1¹/₂ CUPS

2 tablespoons	olive oil
1	small onion, chopped
5 cloves	garlic, crushed
¹/₂ cup	white wine
1 cup	Veal Stock or Rich Brown Chicken Stock (pages 199 and 193)
3 sprigs	fresh thyme
	kosher salt and freshly ground pepper

Heat the olive oil in a medium saucepan over medium heat. Add the onion and garlic and cook, stirring occasionally, until they turn golden brown, 5 to 7 minutes. Add the white wine, raise the heat, and boil until the liquid is thickened and almost syrupy, about 5 minutes.

Add the veal or brown chicken stock and the thyme. Simmer for 15 minutes, or until the *jus* coats the back of a spoon. Season with salt and pepper to taste. Strain and reserve the *jus* until needed.

Brown Butter

Also called *beurre noisette* in French because of its nut-brown color—any darker and you have burned it! The flavor is very special.

½ pound   unsalted butter

Melt the butter in a small saucepan over medium heat and cook until nut brown. Strain through a sieve lined in cheesecloth and set aside until needed.

Red Bell Pepper Sauce

You can follow this same procedure for a yellow or orange bell pepper sauce, and use the three sauces together to have the different colors and flavors on the same plate.

For a more robust and smoky-flavored sauce, grill or sear the peppers over a gas flame until the skin is lightly charred, then put them in a plastic bag to finish the cooking and to loosen the skins before removing them.

6	large red bell peppers
3 tablespoons	olive oil
½ cup	chicken stock
2 tablespoons	unsalted butter
	salt and freshly ground pepper

Preheat the oven to 350°F.

Rub the peppers with the olive oil and put them in a baking dish. Cover the peppers with aluminum foil and cook until soft, about 45 minutes. Remove the peppers from the oven and let them stand, still covered, until just cool enough to handle.

Remove the stalks, seeds, ribs, and skins from the peppers, but reserve all the juices. Puree the peppers with their juices in a food processor and pass through a fine-mesh sieve.

To make the sauce, heat the puree with the chicken stock in a small saucepan. When the puree boils, remove from the heat and whisk in the butter. Season with salt and pepper.

Pizza Dough

1 package (¹/₄ ounce)	dry yeast
1¹/₂ cups	water
¹/₂ cup	olive oil
5 cups	bread flour
2 teaspoons	salt

Dissolve the yeast in the water. Stir in the oil and let stand for 10 minutes.

Mix in half the bread flour and the salt until smooth. Knead by hand or in a mixer with a dough hook attachment on medium speed, adding the rest of the flour gradually, until the dough is smooth and elastic, about 15 minutes. As soon as the dough pulls away from the sides of the bowl or just stops sticking to your hands and the board, stop adding flour.

Put the dough in an oiled bowl and let rise for 1 to 2 hours, or until it is doubled.

Pasta Dough

1 pound	all-purpose flour, plus extra for kneading
4	large whole eggs
2	egg yolks
1 teaspoon	salt
2 tablespoons	olive oil

Put the flour in a bowl, make a well in the center of the flour, and add the eggs, the additional yolks, the salt, and the olive oil. Mix the eggs gradually into the flour.

Gather the dough into a ball, dust with flour, and knead it on a lightly floured surface until the dough is dry, elastic, and smooth. Wrap in a towel or non-smelling plastic wrap and refrigerate for 1 hour.

Cut the dough into pieces and roll out by hand or in a pasta machine. Cut into the shapes you need.

JEREMIAH TOWER

MAKES 4 TO 6 PIZZAS

Ever since, by accident, on the third birthday of Chez Panisse in 1974, we invented the small individual pizza, topped with whatever was in the refrigerator (grilled prawns, a mix of vegetables, smoked fish, chicken mixed with ancho chili mayonnaise), there has been a superb free-for-all with pizza. But it is still the dough that makes a pizza.

JEREMIAH TOWER

MAKES ABOUT 1 POUND

The proportions for this recipe will depend on the type of flour used and the size of the eggs, but 4 ounces of flour to 1 egg plus a yolk is my general rule, and bread flour or good semolina flour is the best.

The secret to making pasta by hand is a long, slow kneading until the texture of the dough is like satin.

Oven-Dried Pears for Roasted Meats, Game, and Poultry

4	pears
1 tablespoon	kosher or sea salt
1 cup	sugar

Whenever a recipe calls for fruit to accompany meat, game, and poultry (like duck with pears), this is the best way I know to bring out the flavors of the fruit, giving a commercial product a whole new lease on life as if it were ripe fruit fresh from a farm in Oregon or Long Island. The process is oven drying, slowly evaporating all that Colorado River irrigation water from the fruit without cooking it.

Preheat the oven to 300°F.

Slice the pears in half lengthwise. Rub each half with a pinch of salt.

Put parchment paper on a tray just large enough to hold the pears and pour the sugar on the paper. There should be a 1/16-inch layer. Put the pear halves cut side down on the sugar and bake for 1 to 2 hours, depending on the ripeness of the fruit. Hard Sekel pears, for example, take 1 1/4 hours.

As soon as the pears are cool enough to handle, remove the cores and stems, and proceed with any recipe that calls for the fruit as a garnish.

VARIATION

Oven-Dried Fruit   Do the same thing with halved apples, peeled pineapple, quinces, plums, apricots (especially, since they tend to be the most ruined by growers), peaches, and figs.

Salt-Preserved Lemons

JEREMIAH TOWER

16	medium lemons, preferably organic
1 cup	sugar
3 cups	kosher salt
10	whole allspice
2 tablespoons	fennel seed
2 tablespoons	black peppercorns
1 tablespoon	cumin seed
1 tablespoon	coriander seed
1 tablespoon	black mustard seed
1	cinnamon stick
5	bay leaves
4 cups	freshly squeezed lemon juice
1 cup	freshly squeezed lime juice

MAKES 16 PRESERVED
LEMONS

Use limes, kumquats (only a week to cure), and other sour citrus as well. And make sure that the spices you use are freshly bought.

Do not make these in small quantities; give some away as presents. Keep for up to 3 months in the refrigerator. To use, squeeze the juice from the lemon back into the jar, remove the seeds, and chop the whole thing.

Roll each lemon around on the table for a minute to release its juices, and then cut an X 2 inches deep at both ends of each lemon.

Mix the sugar and salt together in a bowl. Roll each lemon in the mixture until well coated. Place the lemons in a big sterilized canning jar or other glass container, packing them in fairly tightly. Cover and leave at room temperature for 8 hours.

Mix all the spices, the cinnamon stick, and the bay leaves with the lemon juice and lime juice. Pour over the lemons, making sure that the liquid surrounds all the fruit. Weight down with a plate and can of something so that all the lemons stay submerged. Cover and leave out at room temperature for 1 week, turning the jar every day to evenly distribute the salt, spices, and juices. Then refrigerate for 3 to 4 weeks, again turning the lemons around in the container once a week.

At this point, strain the liquid and pour it back over the lemons. Keep them covered and refrigerated. Use as needed for up to 6 months.

Garlic Puree

MAKES ABOUT 1 CUP

8 heads	fresh young spring garlic
1/4 cup	olive oil
4 sprigs	fresh thyme
	salt and freshly ground pepper

By the mid-eighties, the "roasted garlic" that I introduced to California at Chez Panisse 12 years previously had spread far and wide in the United States. Unfortunately, most of the time it was not understood properly, because chefs were using any old garlic that was available. Roasting older garlic makes an indigestible puree so potent that it might as well be raw. So please use the most glorious garlic of all, which is the first crop in spring—when the cloves are fresh and white with pink and purple streaks through the outer leaves, the stems are green and soft, and the aroma of the garlic is mild and sweet.

Both this spring garlic puree and the poached garlic puree described at right can be held in the refrigerator in a sealed jar for a week.

Note: Instead of making a puree, the roasted garlic heads can be served whole, drizzled with olive oil or melted butter.

Preheat the oven to 300°F.

Rub the garlic heads with the oil. Strew the thyme in a heavy baking dish just large enough to hold the garlic in a single layer. Place the garlic on the thyme and season with salt and pepper. Cover with foil and bake until the garlic cloves are just soft when you squeeze them, 30 to 45 minutes.

Take the garlic out of the baking dish. Squeeze the puree from each clove and mash with a fork, or put them through a food mill to make a puree. Discard the skins. Cover any unused puree tightly and store in the refrigerator for up to a week.

Tip: If you want to make a garlic puree with the more common "dried" fresh garlic (which should be as fresh as possible, firm, and free of mildew), it should be poached first. Take unpeeled cloves and poach them in chicken stock or salted water until soft, about 15 minutes. Then put them through a food mill or sieve to make a mild, white puree for thickening roasting juices; to put on toasted bread, lamb, or chicken; to add to cream for a pasta sauce; or to make garlic soup.

Aromatic Vegetable Mix

1 pound	carrots, peeled, chopped
1 pound	onions, chopped
1 pound	celery stalks, chopped
1	bay leaf, crumbled

Chop the vegetables, mix together, and add the bay leaf.

For meat stocks, cut the vegetables into 2-inch pieces.

For poultry stocks, cut the vegetables into 1-inch pieces.

For fish stocks, cut the vegetables into 1/4-inch pieces.

For braising stocks, cut the vegetables into 1-inch pieces.

For cooking with food for less than 30 minutes, cut the vegetables into 1/8-inch pieces.

Note: When the vegetable mix is to be left in the sauce or served with the dish, it should be cut up quite small, and that is what is meant when you see the word matignon *in books on French classic cooking. You will also see the word* brunoise, *the same mix cut up in 1/8-inch dice, or a mixture of other vegetables like turnip, parsnip, and celery root. If it is to be served with the dish in its final form, is used in a short cooking phase (15 minutes), or if a new mix is cooked and added after the first aromatic one is sieved out of the cooking juices, a small dice mix is used.*

JEREMIAH TOWER

MAKES ABOUT 6 CUPS

Called "an aromatic condiment," this mixture of at least carrot, onion, and celery, and bay leaf perfumes and flavors meats, vegetables (as in braised artichokes) and poultry when cooked with it.

Most every cuisine has its own version: the *soffritto* in Italy (onions, tomatoes, herbs and olive oil), the Puerto Rican and Caribbean version (they add chopped salt pork, ham, and bell peppers), and the *sofregit* or *picada* (almonds, pine nuts, garlic, and parsley ground to a paste) in Catalonia.

Pie Crust or Tart Shell

MAKES ONE 9- TO 10-
INCH ROUND, 1/4 INCH
THICK

2 cups	all-purpose flour, plus additional as needed
1/4 cup	sugar
1/2 teaspoon	salt
1/2 pound	unsalted butter, cut in pieces
1/4 cup	cold water

Combine the flour, the sugar, and the salt in a bowl. Mix the butter quickly into the flour by hand or with the paddle attachment of a mixer until the butter is in small crumbly pieces. Add the water and blend together, gathering the mass into a ball. Wrap in plastic wrap and refrigerate (or freeze) until needed.

Place the pastry on a lightly floured table. If the dough is cold and hard, beat it gently with a rolling pin to soften it. Shape it into a flattened circle. Dust the top with flour, turn over, dust again, and roll out the dough into a 9- or 10-inch round to make a tart shell. Wrap and refrigerate.

Whipped Cream

JEREMIAH TOWER

MAKES 2 CUPS

1 cup	whipping cream
2 tablespoons	superfine (castor) sugar
1/2	vanilla bean, split, seeds scraped out and saved
	salt

Put the cream, sugar, vanilla seeds, and a pinch of salt in a cold, medium-sized bowl and whip the cream until the cream is loosely stiff—or in soft peaks.

If making this in advance, cover the bowl and refrigerate for up to 2 hours. Whip again briefly before serving.

Cinnamon Sugar

JEREMIAH TOWER

MAKES ABOUT 1 CUP

1 cup	granulated sugar
1 tablespoon	ground cinnamon
	salt
1 stick	cinnamon

Mix together the sugar, ground cinnamon, and a pinch of salt. Store in a jar and slide the cinnamon stick down the center of the sugar.

Make sure you use the freshest possible ground cinnamon and store this sugar in a tightly closed jar.

Clarified Butter

JEREMIAH TOWER

MAKES ³/₄ CUPS

1 pound	butter

Melt the butter in the top of a double boiler or over very low heat. When the butter is completely melted, remove from the heat and set aside for 15 minutes. Skim off all the foam from the top. Then spoon off the clear yellow liquid (the clarified butter) and reserve it. Discard the milky liquid in the bottom of the pan.

The main benefit of clarified butter is that, since the milk solids are removed, the butter does not burn so easily when you are using it for frying.

Water-Rendered Fats

JEREMIAH TOWER

MAKES 2 CUPS

2 cups	poultry (chicken, duck, or goose) or ham fat
8 cups	water

Put the fat in the water, bring to a boil, and simmer for 1 hour. Strain and refrigerate. When the fat is congealed, lift it off the water and store in a sealed container. Save the water for soups or stocks.

When animal fats are rendered by frying or baking, they can reach temperatures of up to 500°F, at which point they become oxidized, totally indigestible, a plumber's nightmare (both you and the sink), and deadly.

If they are rendered in water, however, they do not get above the temperature of boiling, do not oxidize, and are light, fresh, full of wonderful flavor, and healthy.

JEREMIAH TOWER

Herb Bundle

MAKES 1 BUNDLE

1	leek, 4 green leaves only, washed
1	stalk celery
1	bay leaf
4 sprigs	fresh parsley
2 sprigs	fresh or dried thyme
2 sprigs	fresh chervil
1 sprig	fresh tarragon

Like the vegetable mix of carrot, onion, and celery that is added to stocks, stews, and braised dishes to lend flavor and "aromatic" structure to the cooking liquids, this bundle of green (or tough outer white) leek leaves, celery leaves, bay leaf, parsley, thyme do the same. They are tied together so the bundle can be easily retrieved after the other ingredients are cooked, and the bundle marries together with the vegetable mix to create an ensemble of flavors rather than a taste of any one of the ingredients. It is very difficult to judge the quantity of dried or fresh herbs for long-cooking dishes, but the flavors of the herbs in this bundle will spread very slowly, so that over a few hours the flavors attenuate and refine.

Open up the leek leaves and wrap them around the gathered-together other ingredients to completely enclose them. Tie up by wrapping the whole thing in 4 or 5 rings of string.

Note: Fresh or dried thyme lends its support to most dishes in a nonassertive or overpowering way, but creates a base for all the other flavors and is essential to the bundle. Other herbs can be included in a bundle, but only if you want that particular flavor, as you adapt the herbs to your cooking and your mood. Marjoram, with its distinctive odor, will stay fairly dominantly with the cooking juices even after they have been cleaned up and turned (reduced) into a sauce. So will the flavors of tarragon, oregano, savory (winter), hyssop (giving a slightly bitter edge to the flavors), and lovage, which riffs off the celery in the bundle, as does the leek with the onions in the vegetable mix.

America's Best Chefs Cook *with* Jeremiah Tower

Index